D1066138

ASK
SUZE®

. . . ABOUT REAL ESTATE

ALSO BY SUZE ORMAN

You've Earned It, Don't Lose It
Suze Orman's Financial Guidebook
The 9 Steps to Financial Freedom
The Courage to Be Rich
The Road to Wealth
The Laws of Money, The Lessons of Life
The Money Book for the Young, Fabulous & Broke
Women & Money

Riverhead Books
a member of
Penguin Group (USA) Inc.
New York
2007

ASK
SUZE®

...ABOUT REAL
ESTATE

SUZE ORMAN

This publication is designed to provide accurate and authoritative information in regard to the subject matter covered. It is published with the understanding that the publisher and author are not engaged in rendering legal, accounting, or other professional services. If legal advice or other professional advice, including financial, is required, the services of a competent professional person should be sought.

While the author has made every effort to provide accurate telephone numbers and Internet addresses at the time of publication, neither the publisher nor the author assumes any responsibility for errors, or for changes that occur after publication.

Ask Suze® is a federally registered mark owned by Suze Orman.

People First, Then Money, Then Things™ is a trademark owned by Suze Orman.

Certified Financial Planner® is a federally registered mark owned by the Certified Financial Planner Board of Standards, Inc.

The term Realtor® is a collective membership mark owned by the National Association of Realtors® and refers to a real estate agent who is a member thereof.

RIVERHEAD BOOKS
a member of
Penguin Group (USA) Inc.
375 Hudson Street
New York, NY 10014

Copyright © 2000, 2004, 2007 by The Suze Orman Revocable Trust
All rights reserved. This book, or parts thereof, may not
be reproduced in any form without permission.
Published simultaneously in Canada

ISBN 978-1-59448-963-1

Printed in the United States of America
1   3   5   7   9   10   8   6   4   2

Book design by Deborah Kerner and Claire Vaccaro

ASK SUZE®

. . . ABOUT REAL ESTATE

THE DOOR TO MORE

A home is one of life's most significant resources. A home is the place where you live, of course, but it's also an investment that can bring you satisfaction and security for years to come. Becoming a homeowner can also be a gigantic step toward financial freedom.

If you've been thinking about buying a first home, are actively hunting for a new home, or simply want to understand more about the opportunities and pitfalls involved in becoming a homeowner, read this chapter carefully. Millions of homes are bought and sold each year, but too many buyers and sellers are unaware of the important variables to look for—and look out for—in the process. They let banks, realtors, and mortgage brokers make decisions for them, often to their detriment. Don't let this happen to you.

The questions and answers below will help you think through the issues involved in buying or selling a home. These include figuring out what kind of house you can truly afford, which type of mortgage will serve you best in different economic environments, the factors that may affect the value of your investment in your home, how to hold your title, and how to measure tax benefits. I hope you will also get a sense of the tremendous security and freedom that come with owning a home free and clear.

To Rent or Buy?

I pay a very low rent, but everyone tells me that I should buy a home. What do you think?
Once upon a time, your decision would have been simple. For our parents and their parents, owning a home almost always made better sense than renting, in large part because mortgage payments were often equal to or smaller than the rents they paid. People tended to live in the same house for 30 years, so the immediate, large expenses associated with buying a home could be amortized over a long period of time. Today, our culture has become far more mobile; in order to be sure that ownership makes sense for you, you must think about how long you will live in a home and have a clear sense of whether property values are moving up or down in the area where you'd like to live.

If you're young, have no idea where you will be living three years from now, are not in need of a tax deduction, and pay less in rent than you would pay for a mortgage, property taxes, and insurance on a similar house or apartment, renting may be preferable for now.

If, on the other hand, you know you will live in the same house for three to five years, believe that real estate prices are on the rise, have money available for a down payment, and have found a home you like with a mortgage, property taxes, and insurance you can afford, then owning is the way to go.

***I really don't have the desire to own a home, but I do
have the money. Should I continue to rent or buy?***

If you can afford a down payment and monthly mortgage payments and expenses, you probably would benefit financially if
you bought a home. But you've already answered the first
question every potential home buyer should ask himself or
herself, which is: *Do I want to own a home?* If not, don't buy,
because home ownership is a big responsibility. Many long-
time renters are surprised by how much time and money is
required to keep a house and property running smoothly and
looking good. If you decide to keep renting, however, invest
your savings so that you can easily purchase a home should
your feelings change.

***A friend told me the tax break for owning a home
always makes renting a bad deal, tax-wise. Is that
true?***

The federal tax break your friend is talking about allows
homeowners to deduct the annual amount of the interest they
pay on their mortgage loans from their income for tax purposes. This can indeed be a great savings, if your mortgage-
interest payments are greater than the standard deduction
allowed by the federal government. Before you decide to buy,
calculate the tax break you'll receive on your yearly mortgage
interest payments, and be sure that the deduction will exceed
the current standard deduction. Chances are good that it will,
since real estate prices, and therefore the amounts of mortgage
loans, have risen so much in recent years.

As a homeowner, you may be able to take advantage of
other tax benefits, such as a deduction for your property taxes,
but the mortgage interest deduction is what most people have
in mind when they say that owning makes for a better tax deal
than renting.

What is the current standard federal deduction?

The standard deduction varies according to your filing status, your age, whether you are blind, and whether you can be claimed as a dependent on another taxpayer's return. The basic standard deductions for the 2006 tax year are as follows:

- Single: $5,150
- Head of Household: $7,550
- Married, filing a joint return: $10,300
- Married, filing a separate return: $5,150

(Please note: These are the most current available figures at the time of writing. They are likely to increase for the tax year 2007, with the deduction for married, filing jointly, increasing according to the Jobs and Growth Tax Relief Reconciliation Act of 2003.)

You said that renting may be wiser if I don't know where I'll be living during the next few years. What difference does it make how long I plan to live in a home?

When you buy or sell a piece of real estate, you pay a number of fees up front that are collectively known as closing costs—so called because they are due from both the buyer and the seller at the time the title to the property is transferred and the deal is closed. These fees can easily cost both buyer and seller several thousand dollars, and that's in addition to the possible costs of paying a realtor to help you buy or sell, plus moving and renovating costs, etc. If you are going to be in your home for fewer than three years, your home may not increase enough in value to cover all these expenses, and you could actually lose money if and when you have to sell. In an ordinary market, you should plan to live in your home for three to five years or longer.

I've been thinking about buying, but I feel that my romantic status might be changing over the next year or two. Should I buy now, or continue to rent until I know for sure?

The question of whether you will require the same amount of living space and the same kinds of amenities in the next few years is an important one. If you are a single person, a one-bedroom condo may seem ideal now, but if you hope to get married and start a family in the next few years, you'll need more space pretty quickly. Life changes make for subtle differences. For a couple that is newly married and without any children, buying a great house in a not-so-great school district might seem sensible; but if the couple has children later or tries to sell the house to people with children, they may discover that the house they bought was not the best buy overall. The goal is to think long-term and to try to evaluate what your requirements will be three, five, or ten years from now. Until you're able to do this, you should probably continue to rent or stay in the home you currently own.

I'm afraid that I will have trouble maintaining a home. Does that come into play when I'm debating buying vs. renting?

Being physically able to maintain your home, regardless of your age, is an important consideration. Owning a home is a lot of work. Senior citizens who are thinking about purchasing a home should consider whether they would be most comfortable with the amenities that a full-service apartment complex or condominium community can offer. Younger men and women who do a lot of business traveling might also find apartment living more convenient. If you cannot maintain a house yourself, you must include home maintenance costs in your financial estimates when deciding if you can afford to own a home. Plan ahead. I suggest putting at least $75 a month into a maintenance fund.

FIRST STEPS TOWARD BUYING A HOME

Once you start thinking about owning a piece of real estate, it can become an all-consuming passion. It's during the initial excitement about buying a home that most people make their first mistake. Before figuring out what they can afford, they drive through the areas in which they want to live, looking for houses with FOR SALE signs. They jot down the phone numbers of real estate agents selling those houses. They place a few calls, just out of curiosity, and before they know it—and before they've worked out their own budget—they've made dates to take a look at what's on the market. This is the usual sequence—and, if you allow yourself to follow it, you can find yourself in over your head. Here are the questions you need to ask and answer before you begin shopping for a home.

CALCULATING THE SIZE OF THE MORTGAGE PAYMENT YOU CAN AFFORD

I saved eight months' worth of expenses for an emergency fund. I would like to use this money for a down payment on a home. Is this a wise thing to do?

Unless you are convinced that you are immune from emergencies, I don't think this is a very good idea. Emergency funds should be a permanent part of your financial picture; that's how you will always have the ability to weather any unforeseen problem.

Let's say you use the money for a down payment. Next you'll tell me that you need to furnish your great new home. So you are going to run up some hefty credit card balances. Everything seems great until that unforeseen disaster occurs: You get laid off. You now have no job, and no emergency fund, and no ability to tap your credit card for a cash advance, because you are currently at your maximum balances. Tell me, how will you pay your mortgage now? I fear that you could lose your house. And I am not being overly cautious; as I write this book, there are more than a million foreclosures predicted for 2006 alone.

So that's why I want you to always have an eight-month emergency fund. Another option is to have access to cash advances on your credit cards that are equal to eight months of your living costs. But this is far from ideal, since you will be stuck paying high interest rates if you ever do need to tap those advances in an emergency.

What are the most important things to consider before I buy a home?

Perhaps the most important consideration is what your financial limits are. The following is a list of financial realities to think about.

How much cash will you be able to come up with for a down payment?

Will you have the additional cash necessary to pay the closing costs?

What is your monthly income, before and after taxes?

Apart from the money for a down payment, how much money have you saved? (Include everything—savings accounts, retirement accounts, and any other key assets.)

How much debt do you have? (Again, include everything—credit cards, student loans, and/or car loans.)

How much do you spend each month paying off your debts?

How long have you been in your current job?

What does your credit history look like?

What are the costs of houses in the area(s) that you are thinking about living in?

How much are average property taxes in the area(s) you are thinking about living in?

What are current interest rates, and are they projected to get lower or higher in the near future?

How much does homeowner's insurance cost for houses of the general size and location that interest you?

What is the very first step I should take before I go and look at houses?

Before you do anything, you must know how much you can afford to spend. As a homeowner, you will have many more expenses than you had as a renter. Before you fall in love with a house and talk yourself into buying something that you may not be able to comfortably afford, I want you to start out knowing exactly how much you can pay and why.

Figuring out what you can afford is simple, as long as you are honest with yourself about your income and financial obligations. Just follow the steps below.

1. Calculate your current net monthly income after taxes, Social Security contributions, retirement contributions, and all other automatic withdrawals from your paycheck. Write that figure here:
   Figure 1: _____

2. Total the monthly payments on all your debts—

include car payments, credit card payments, personal loans, and student loans. (Don't include mortgage payments or rent.) Be honest! Write the total here:

Figure 2: _____

If Figure 2 equals more than 30 percent of Figure 1, stop right here. (Multiply Figure 1 by 0.3 to get 30 percent.) You are not currently in a financial position to own a home comfortably. You must first reduce your debt.

3. Find the sum that represents your monthly living expenses. Include food, transportation, gasoline, haircuts, dental, education, utilities, insurance—in other words, any regular bills that you pay, *excluding* the amount of your current rent or mortgage payments but *including* your debt payments (Figure 2). Write that figure here:

   Figure 3: _____

4. Subtract Figure 3 from Figure 1. Write the result here:

   Figure 4: _____

   Figure 4 is the maximum monthly amount you currently can afford to spend on a mortgage payment plus property taxes, homeowner's insurance, maintenance, possible PMI costs, and the other hidden costs of home ownership.

   Keep in mind that this formula does not account for the tax savings that owning a home will confer. You will want to figure those savings into your monthly calculations before you shop for a home. Since you will likely save on both your federal and state taxes, be sure to consult a tax adviser.

5. Subtract 35 percent from Figure 4 (multiply Figure 4 by 0.65). Write the result here:

   Figure 5: _____

Figure 5 is the highest comfortable monthly amount you can currently afford for a mortgage payment alone.

I've heard people say that after calculating the size of the mortgage payments that I can afford, I still need to "play house." What does that mean?

Playing house is a way of trying new financial situations on for size. This is how it works: Open up a brand-new savings account. Remember, this is something you want to do well *before* you are really serious about buying a home. Set a date once a month—for instance, the 15th. For the next six months, on that date, I want you to deposit into your new account the exact difference between what your current housing costs (rent, or the total payments you are making on the home you currently own) and the amount you project you will have to pay on your new home.

For example, let's say that your are renting, and it costs you $1,500 a month to rent. The house you want to buy will cost you $3,500 a month (including mortgage payment, PMI, property insurance, taxes, utilities, and maintenance). You must deposit the difference between the two ($3,500-$1,500, or $2,000 a month) into the new savings account, no later than the date you set.

Or say that you currently own a home and want to buy a bigger home. Your current total monthly payments come to $3,000, and your new home will cost you $6,200 a month. To play house, you must deposit the difference between the two ($6,200 - $3,000, or $3,200 a month) into a savings account no later than the date you set.

These examples feature the minimum costs. They don't include all the expenses, such as lawn maintenance and snow removal. So if you really want to do a thorough job, you should also figure out which of those other expenses you will have to pay and how much they will cost you.

After doing this for six months, evaluate how making those higher payments while playing house has affected your lifestyle. If you've made all the payments comfortably and on time, you know that you can truly afford this particular home right now. Better yet, you have already accumulated funds to put toward increasing your down payment, helping you with moving costs or closing costs, or even doing a few small renovations on the new home!

If, on the other hand, you missed payments or were late in making any, you cannot afford the house you were thinking about buying quite yet. Instead, look to see the monthly payment that would have been comfortable for you, and try that. Maybe the solution is to consider a smaller house or a larger down payment. Nevertheless, you may just have to wait until your finances improve. The good news is that you now know how much you realistically can afford at this time *without* having lost any money in finding out. You should also have a nice sum of money in your savings account that will help you achieve your future goals.

I know I will save money on taxes with a mortgage interest deduction. How can I get that tax savings to help me pay my bills month to month?

If you are working for an employer, notify your employer that you have bought a home and request an increase in the number of your exemptions. (As of 2006, each exemption removes $3,300 a year from your taxable income.) If you do this, your employer will withhold less money from your paycheck for taxes, and you will have use of that money every month. Please consult a tax professional first, however, so that you are absolutely sure your employer is withholding the right amount of tax.

How much can I expect to pay in homeowner's insurance?

A quick way to figure out your monthly homeowner's insurance costs is to multiply $35 times each $100,000 of the value of your house. For example, if you have a home valued at $200,000, you would multiply 35×2 to get a monthly homeowner's insurance cost of $70. This is a rough approximation. To get an exact quote, you will need to speak to a homeowner's insurance provider. The cost of insurance varies according to state, the price of the house, and the amount of coverage you'll need to feel comfortable. Call a local insurance agent and get an estimate on the house you wish to buy.

How do I figure out what my yearly property taxes will be?

When you sign a contract to buy a house, you get a title report that includes the most recent real estate tax information on the property. Though tax rates can go up from year to year, the most recent figures from the title report will be a good indicator, unless the price of the house has risen dramatically since the last annual tax assessment. For advance warning, ask your real estate agent for an estimate or call the local tax assessment office in the area where you want to buy.

My husband says if we are approved for a mortgage, we can afford the house. Is he right?

If your husband thinks the bank will guide you, he's wrong. Every loan that has ever gone into foreclosure or bankruptcy was approved by a bank. A loan officer qualified those borrowers, and then something went wrong. To avoid having something go wrong with your home purchase, make sure *you* feel comfortable with the monthly mortgage and other payments you'll have to make—in other words, decide for yourself what you can and can't afford. Remember, if you get in over your head, it will probably not hurt the banker—it will hurt you.

Please note that a mortgage may seem to be a loan that you use to pay for your home, but technically it is a lien on your home by means of which a lender secures a loan for you. It is what's known as a secured loan. If you fail to pay back the mortgage, the lender has the ability to foreclose on the property.

What is foreclosure?

Foreclosure is the legal process by which a lender assumes a borrower's property rights in lieu of payment of a mortgage— and by which the borrower who has failed to pay loses his or her rights and interest in the property. In other words, in foreclosure the lender takes the home away from you and, typically, sells it at auction in order to recover the loan.

THE DOWN PAYMENT

Once you've arrived at the size of the mortgage you can afford, let's turn to the next item that will influence the price of the home you can buy: how much money you have for a down payment. A down payment is paid up front and is usually expressed as a percentage of the purchase price. Below are the questions you'll need to ask and answer about down payments.

Does it matter how large a down payment I make when purchasing a home?

Lenders generally prefer that borrowers put down 20 percent of the total purchase price of the home. Thus the traditional down payment on a $200,000 home is $40,000. But don't panic if you don't have 20 percent to put down. Some lenders are willing to accept down payments as small as 0–3 percent of the purchase price. A smaller down payment will come at a cost to you, however, which I'll discuss in detail when we talk about mortgages. Other lending programs (such as Veterans Administration and Federal Housing Administration loans) and alternative arrangements (i.e., having the seller carry the bank loan) are possible in cases where a standard bank loan isn't feasible.

I understand the concept of the down payment, but I don't have a lot of cash. Where can I find the money?
Finding cash for the down payment is often the biggest hurdle people face when buying a home. If you've gone through all the obvious possibilities—savings, investment accounts, bonuses at work—and are still short, consider the following options, but know that using them will come at a price.

- A loan against your 401(k)
- A withdrawal of up to $10,000 from your traditional IRA/Roth IRA. (This withdrawal from a traditional IRA is subject to income tax but not a penalty if you meet the specific first-time buyer definition—but be careful, because income tax may eat up a good portion of the withdrawal. Roth IRAs have special rules here as well, so please get tax advice before taking any steps.)

Naturally, you should think long and hard before you use money from your retirement accounts, because these represent important components of your long-term savings plan; tapping into them them will certainly interfere with their growth and diminish your nest egg. (To learn more about the pros and cons of borrowing from retirement savings, as well as the rules that apply, please see *Ask Suze . . . About Debt.*)

Many employers will let you borrow as much as 50 percent of the money you have in your 401(k), up to a ceiling of $50,000. With a traditional IRA, you can *withdraw* up to $10,000, but this is not a loan; you will have to pay income taxes on that money.

With a Roth IRA, you are permitted to withdraw any portion of your original contribution at any time. Your withdrawal of contributions is tax- and penalty-free. If you also withdraw part of your gains, using the first-time homeowner provision, and are under age 59½, you will owe ordinary income taxes on the earnings part of the withdrawal but no penalty.

If I do not have 20 percent to put down (I have about 10 percent), but I can get a mortgage and can easily afford the monthly mortgage payments, should I go ahead and buy the house anyway?

In most cases, yes. You can feel especially confident if a) you believe you will live in the home for at least three to five years, and b) the value of the home you want to buy has not been overly inflated by a booming real estate market.

Which is more important—a down payment of 20 percent or the money to make the mortgage payments?

In my opinion, having the money to pay the monthly mortgage bill and meet other ongoing expenses, such as property taxes and insurance, is more important. You may be able to scrape together the money for a down payment, especially if it's less than 20 percent of the price of the house. But if you fall behind on your mortgage payments or other obligations, you will not enjoy, and may even lose, your home. Don't become "house-poor." Make sure you will be able to enjoy your home—and life's other pleasures—*after* you move in.

CREDIT HISTORY

Once you have cleared the two big hurdles of determining the size of the mortgage you can afford and identifying the source of your down payment, there's a final step to take before going out to look for a home in your price range. The last step will be to qualify for a mortgage, which may mean working on your credit.

Please see the sections on credit reports and FICO score in *Ask Suze . . . About Debt,* and thoroughly review the information about obtaining and correcting your credit report and improving your FICO score. Any lender you approach will perform a credit check, and you will want to be sure that you are prepared to pass the test.

Can you give me an example of how a FICO score can reduce my mortgage?

A great credit report can snag a high FICO score. And that can translate into saving thousands of dollars on your loan costs. For example, let's say you are looking for a $216,000 30-year fixed-rate mortgage. If you nab a great FICO score (760–850) you could qualify for a 5.95 percent interest rate that would give you an $1,289 monthly mortgage. Over the life of the loan you would pay $247,863 in interest. Now let's look at the other end of the spectrum: You earn a very low FICO score (620–659 is the low range), which means your mortgage rate is a far costlier 7.26 percent. Your monthly mortgage payment balloons to $1,477, and you'll pay more than $315,458 in interest over the life of the loan. This translates into $67,595 more in interest simply because lenders think you're a credit risk. To see how to get a lower interest rate, please see the information on FICO scores in *Ask Suze . . . About Debt.*

Before I go to a lender to find out if I can qualify for a mortgage, should I find out what my credit report looks like?

You should *always* know what your credit report and FICO score look like. If you don't, write for a copy at least six months before you begin looking for a home. That way, you'll have enough time to correct any errors.

Is there a website that will give me a rough idea whether my credit and FICO score are good or bad before I pay for a credit report or apply for a mortgage?

Yes. You can get some general information that explains what goes into a credit score at *www.myfico.com*, but the actual score will cost you a nominal fee.

If I am using a real estate agent or mortgage broker, can he or she correct my credit report for me?

No, a real estate agent or mortgage broker will not correct your credit report. If there are mistakes on your report, however, many agents and brokers *will* help you draft a letter to your prospective lender explaining why the report is not accurate. But please get to your credit report before your prospective lender does, and clear up or annotate any inaccuracies you find.

If my credit history is less than perfect, is there anything I should do before I apply for a mortgage?

If you think you will be applying for a mortgage in the near future, please do the following:

Keep your credit card balances as low as possible. Do *not* have your cards maxed out when you apply for a mort-

gage. Be punctual with all your payments. Now is not
the time to be even one day late.

Do not apply for a low-interest-rate credit card at this
time.

Do not switch multiple small balances from your high-
interest-rate cards to one low-interest-rate card. Instead,
try to pay down as many card balances as possible.

Why should you take these precautions? When mortgage
lenders look at your credit report, one of the things they'll
check for is your credit limit—the maximum amount of
money you can charge against your credit cards. If you have a
Visa card with a $5,000 limit, a MasterCard with a $10,000
limit, and a Discover card with a $3,000 limit, a mortgage
lender will view this as the potential to create an additional
$18,000 debt. Try not to let your maximum potential debt
grow. Also, you don't want to apply for any new cards, to prevent unnecessary credit inquiries on your report. A lender will
wonder why you are seeking additional credit.

I checked my FICO score, and it is lower than I thought. If I have a low credit score, can I still shop around for a mortgage?

Yes, you can, but it would be to your advantage to work on
improving your FICO score before looking for a mortgage. A
higher FICO score could save you thousands on your mortgage. If you can't wait, then log on to *moving.com*, click on
Mortgage Quotes, and select Poor Under Estimated Credit
Rating. This is a mortgage referral site that will give you mortgage quotes according to your credit rating. The poorer your
credit score, the more you will have to shop around.

FINDING THE RIGHT HOUSE AND LOCATION

Now that you have been armed with accurate information about what you can afford, it's time to look for a home. When shopping for real estate, the old saying *is* true: The three most important variables are location, location, and location. The ongoing value of your home is very strongly determined by— you guessed it—its location.

Should I get a real estate agent from the start, or should I look around on my own?

If you are knowledgeable about a region, start by driving around. Identify neighborhoods in which you might want to live. Then call a real estate agent who specializes in the neighborhoods you've chosen. However, if you are moving to a new area and don't have a clear sense of where you want to live, you can speed up the house-hunting process by asking an agent (or agents) to take you around. This will clue you in to how well an agent knows the areas she or he represents.

Even at the very beginning of the process, it is important to work with an agent you feel you can communicate with. Choose carefully, for this person can control the properties you see and can influence how effectively you bid on the properties you like. Make sure he or she answers your questions clearly and is available when needed.

Is looking for a house on the Web a good idea?

I think using the Web is an excellent way to *start* looking for a house or apartment. Browse the Web to get an idea of available properties and prices in your region. If you like what you see, then visit in person. A site that I think you will find useful is *www.realtor.com.*

When is the best time of day to look at a home in person?

Visit a prospective home at as many different times of day as you can, and on weekdays and weekends, too. Here's why. Imagine you find a house that you love. You drive by on a Sunday afternoon and stop in on the following Wednesday afternoon. During both visits, the neighborhood seems peaceful and quiet. You buy the house, and on your first Monday morning there, at 7 A.M., horns blare and tires screech. It happens that your street is a good rush-hour shortcut around the town's business district. There go your peaceful mornings and dinner hours.

Some reliable sources of information about the character of a neighborhood, including whether or not it's safe, are the seller's neighbors. If you see people gardening, playing with their children, or pulling into or out of their driveways, ask them a few questions about the street and the surrounding dwellers. They'll often be very candid.

We've found the perfect neighborhood. What should we look for in a house?

First, look beyond the apparent charms of a house. Many people, especially first-time home buyers, fall in love with a single quality in a house—a new kitchen, for example, or even a lovely pair of French doors leading into a garden—and neglect to consider the whole package. Bring a notepad, walk through every room, and make a list of problems. If you don't see anything that is damaged, inadequate, or displeasing, you may not be looking hard enough. Return with a friend, tour the house or apartment separately, and compare notes afterward. I guarantee that each of you will have seen a different house.

What are some common problems that buyers tend to overlook?

To be sure you are not buying someone else's problems, make a list of the following things to look for or do.

Turn on all the water faucets and let them run; check the water pressure, and make sure that the hot water is plentiful.

Flush all the toilets.

Make sure that the appliances (refrigerator and freezer, air conditioners, dishwashers, washers, and dryers) are in working order and are not more than ten years old.

Check all outlets, lights, and light switches.

If you're looking at an old house, ask the seller (or the real estate agent, if you don't meet the seller) when the plumbing and electrical systems were last replaced or repaired.

Turn on everything at once and see what happens—if lights dim when the air conditioner and the washing machine are running, you'll probably want an electrical engineer to take a look before you contract to buy the house.

Ask the seller or agent how old the roof is and whether it has ever been replaced.

Return after a heavy rainstorm to look for leaks inside, and test the basement for dampness. If it is damp, and if you're still interested in the house, inform the inspector.

Remember that thoroughness is the byword of a happy purchase.

Does it matter how the neighborhood is zoned?

It certainly does. A friend of mine bought a beautiful home in a resort town with a backyard overlooking unused farmland. A year later, the land was sold to a restaurant developer. She spent thousands of dollars putting up fences and planting mature hedges to block out her new neighbor. The lesson is simple: Ask about the zoning laws in the area surrounding your prospective new home.

We're moving to a town we selected because one of the schools is rated the best in the state. My husband says this is good for resale value. Is this true?

Yes. Most young families want to live in highly rated school districts, and buying in one will help secure the resale value of your home, even during tough times. Be careful, however, that the home you're buying is really *in* a good school district and not merely *near* one. Again, the seller's neighbors can save you some heartache if you take the time to ask them a few questions.

BUYING A CO-OP/CONDOMINIUM

What is the difference between a cooperative apartment and a condominium?

Co-ops and condos are both typically units in apartment buildings or townhouse developments in which the individual dwellings are occupied by separate owners. The primary difference between the two is in how the owners hold their individual apartments.

In co-ops, residents do not own the actual apartments they live in. The cooperative corporation owns the building, and residents own shares of the corporation, which are allocated according to the size and value of their respective apartments. As a tenant/shareholder in a co-op, you hold a proprietary lease that allows you to occupy the apartment. A co-op board approves the purchase or sale of shares and usually exerts control over issues of home renovation and the operation and maintenance of the building. It can be difficult to get a mortgage loan on a co-op, and it's impossible to get a reverse mortgage. Cooperatives are common only in big cities.

Buying a condominium is more like buying a house. You are purchasing a piece of real estate—your unit—that is part of a larger building or development, and you are also buying a share of the common areas. Generally, in condominiums you do not need anyone's permission to sell or lease your unit.

In both cases, residents pay monthly fees for the general upkeep of the building and for any staff wages. These fees are called maintenance fees in co-ops and common charges in condos.

I'm a city dweller and most of the homes for sale in my price range are either co-ops or condominiums. Is there anything special to know?

Yes. Before you start looking for a co-op or condo, be aware of two important distinctions between buying a single, detached home on the one hand and a co-op or a condo on the other. The most important difference is that the mortgage interest rate you pay may be higher when you buy a co-op or condo. With these, the theory goes, a lender is taking on a larger risk because the value of your apartment (your "unit") depends partially on the maintenance, condition, and operation of the other units and common areas in the building. When you have your particular unit inspected, ask the engineer to examine the building's common areas and systems. This additional service will probably add to the inspection bill but will be valuable information should you decide to purchase.

Second, and this is a big one, if you buy a co-op you will need to adjust your total monthly payment to include the monthly maintenance charge, which incorporates property taxes as well as fees for general building upkeep and the employment of any staff. With a condominium, you will pay your taxes individually but will owe a monthly common charge for the operation and maintenance of the building's common areas.

BUYER'S AGENTS

More and more real estate agents are being paid on a commission basis. The typical commission on residential real estate is 6 percent of the selling price. The higher the sale price, the more the real estate agent makes. Since the agent's commission is based on the sale price and is paid by the seller, all agents effectively work for the seller.

But a new breed of agent, called a buyer's agent, is entering the marketplace, and he or she works for the buyer. A buyer's agent is paid a percentage of the selling price of the home at the time of the closing and is generally paid by the listing, or selling, agent from that agent's commission.

If I use a buyer's agent, what should he or she do for me?

In general, a buyer's agent should identify and show you a selection of homes that meet your needs and budget. Once you have decided on a home you like, he or she should research the property, help you decide on the price you should pay, and make an offer to the seller or the seller's agent on your behalf. A buyer's agent should also help you to determine how much house you can really afford. All of the above should be written in a contract between you and your agent, which should also include the length of time the agent will represent you and how the fees will be paid. The terms can be specified to meet your needs, so ask for what you want.

If you want to find a buyer's agent, start by looking at the website *www.naeba.com.* The initials stand for the National Association of Exclusive Buyer Agents.

If I want to live in a very desirable area, where houses are sold almost before they are listed, will getting a buyer's agent help?

In an area that's highly competitive, using a buyer's agent won't guarantee you a home, but it will help ensure that you will pay a fair market price for the home you get.

How much should I expect to save by using a buyer's agent?

According to the National Association of Realtors, a buyer's agent may save you about 8 to 10 percent of the cost of the home.

COMPARABLE MARKET ANALYSIS (CMA)

How do I know how much I should pay for a home?

Obtain a comparable market analysis (CMA) from your real estate agent. A CMA provides a comparison of the prices of homes currently on the market and homes sold within the last month and within five blocks of the home you want to buy. Information provided in a CMA on comparable properties should include square footage, number of rooms, location, and size of the property.

If I am not working with a real estate agent, can I get a CMA online?

You can, but be sure you know how to interpret it. That said, check out *www.homepricecheck.com* or *www.dataquick.com* (the latter will cost you a few bucks, but I think it's worth it). If you find a service on your own, make sure that it offers a CMA report for the area in which you are looking for a home.

PREAPPROVED LOANS

I've been told that before I even go to look at homes, I should either be prequalified or preapproved for a mortgage. What do you think?

A prequalification is just an informal review of your circumstances by a lender. A prequalification letter isn't binding and doesn't mean much. On the other hand, to get a preapproval letter requires an in-depth investigation by a potential lender. In competitive housing markets, you'll probably need to be armed with a preapproval letter from your lender. Such a letter provides the seller and the real estate agent with proof of your eligibility and seriousness as a potential buyer. This can be especially helpful if you are dealing with a seller who needs to move quickly. Also, in a tight market where houses are sold the day they are listed, a preapproval letter might keep you in the game.

What exactly is the difference between being prequalified and preapproved for a mortgage?

Preapproval specifically authorizes you to receive a particular mortgage amount for a specific period of time prior to your finding the property you want. *Prequalification* is merely an informal, nonbinding assessment of your financial status. With a preapproval letter you are a cash buyer. This is very attractive to a seller, who doesn't want to worry about whether your loan application will be rejected after he or she takes the house off the market. While it certainly makes you an appealing buyer in a tight market, don't get a preapproval without thinking the mortgage deal through carefully. You need to do the same kind of research and comparison-shopping you would do for any mortgage. Also, a mortgage preapproval can require you to pay a fee up front. It is good only for a specified period of time—for example, 30 days—and if you don't use it, you will lose the money you spent on the fee.

When preapproving people, our lender estimates the borrowers' housing costs at 35 percent of their gross income. My mom says I should never spend a penny more than 25 percent. Who's right?

Your mom and your lender are not the only ones arguing this point. Twenty years ago, 25 percent of gross income was the standard housing-expense figure recommended by most lenders and financial advisers. But as real estate prices have risen in many parts of the country, the recommended percentage has edged higher. What does this mean in terms of cold, hard cash? Let's say you and your partner make a combined gross income of $60,000. Using the 25 percent rule, you could afford $15,000 per year, or $1,250 per month, for your housing costs. If you go with your lender's guideline of 35 percent, you could afford $21,000 per year, or $1,750 per month. That's a difference of $500 per month, enough to create a dramatic difference in the home you buy and also in the way you live. If you want to use the gross income formula to decide what you can afford, I suggest you use the percentage used by the FHA: 31 percent of your gross income.

In my view, however, the whole "gross income" debate is antiquated. Today's worker brings home a check that is very different from his or her parents'. I recommend that you calculate your spending limits based on your real, or net, income. Your lender's figure of 35 percent may stretch you to your limit and leave you without a safety net. Your mom's advice, on the other hand, may be too conservative or constraining.

Your object is to *keep* the home you buy, and the best way to do that is to make sure your total monthly payments fit into your monthly budget.

How much debt can I have and still be preapproved for a mortgage?

As a general rule, lenders look askance at anyone who must spend more than 36 percent of gross income each month to pay back debt. This includes *all* debt—credit card payments, student loans, car loans, and outstanding bills, in addition to monthly mortgage costs, homeowner's insurance, and property taxes. If you have debt that you cannot pay down because you lack cash to do so, you probably have not only too much debt to get a mortgage but also not enough cash to make a down payment. If this is the case, you may be heading for trouble.

Does the length of time I have worked at my job matter when I am getting preapproved for a mortgage?

Yes. Though your recent job history is not the most important item on your mortgage application, lenders do like to see that you have been either at your current job or in your current line of work for at least two years. This suggests that you are fairly stable. But don't panic if you have recently made a job change—all it means is that, if the lender requests it, you may need to provide additional information about your job.

WHEN TO BUY OR SELL

Is now a good to time to buy or to sell?

First, let's all agree that your home is not simply an investment. Your home is a place of security; it is where you live. You don't live in a stock or a mutual fund. So always look at real estate in terms of whether it is the right house for you and your family to live in.

With that bit of perspective, here's a tip for you to use so you can understand what is going on in your real estate market. I want you to check the real estate sales info in your local newspaper; most papers carry a list of recent transactions at least once a week. I want you to track two important trends. First, are homes selling for more than their asking price, or less than their asking price? And are homes selling quickly or slowly? Keep track of this for a few weeks and you are bound to see a pattern.

If the trend in your area is that homes are taking longer and longer to sell and are selling for less than the asking price, then you most likely are in what is known as a *buyer's market.* That's great if you in fact are looking to buy. Since market conditions are in your favor, you can be a serious bargainer. I wouldn't hesitate to go in and make a bid that's 20 percent below the asking price. After some negotiating, I bet you'll come away with a good deal. But, of course, since many of us already own a home, if we go to buy another one it may mean we need to sell our existing home. And if you're a seller in a buyer's market, well, obviously the opposite is true: You're going to need to negotiate and bargain. Or if that doesn't float your boat, then you need to decide if you really want to sell in a buyer's market.

MAKING A BID

My wife and I found a house we want to make a bid on.
We have never gotten this far before, and the real
estate agent is telling us to bid 25 percent below the
asking price. Is she right?

I don't like cut-and-dried rules like this one. The key to making a good bid is to come from a position of strength, and the first step in creating a position of strength is to see as many houses in your purchasing area as you possibly can. Even if you find the house you want on the first try, go out and see more just to establish the basic price range in your area. If you see two or three houses that you believe should be about the same price as the one you like but are $50,000 less, you know the seller's asking price is well above market. After you've thoroughly assessed the market value of the area, come up with a bid based on the limits you set before you started to look. Depending on the area and the volume of sales, I'd generally come in below the asking price. How much below depends on the market. In very fast-moving markets in the late 90s, a fairly priced home could sell to the first bidder who matched the asking price, or it could even sell for more than the asking price. In a slower market, where houses take on average two or more months to sell, the seller might accept a bid as low as 25 percent below the asking price. It depends on the markets.

I've made my final bid, and it's $5,000 short of what the
sellers are asking. Nobody else seems very interested,
but the seller won't budge. What can I do to bridge this
gap without going over my limit?

Remain unemotional—if you get the house, great; if you don't, there will be other houses. Don't be afraid to move on. Remember, there are many houses you can buy, but the seller has only one house to sell. That said, it doesn't hurt to ask the real estate agent to take a percentage point or more less on the sale, thus creating a savings to pass on to you. This sometimes works in slower markets, where the seller and the agent are more invested in the sale than you are. Try to cash in on that investment.

We're in the middle of a bidding war over our dream house. We're about to go beyond our predetermined maximum. The real estate agent feels we could carry the extra $50,000 of debt, but I'm not 100 percent sure. What should we do?

Sometimes buyers get hit with an irrational sense of urgency—"This is my dream house and I'll do anything to get it!" If you catch yourself thinking this, be aware that you may be getting yourself into financial trouble. You established your limit in a rational frame of mind; that's why figuring out your limit before you look is critical. There are many other good, affordable homes that can make you happy. Keep on looking.

The real estate market in my area is still going crazy. By the time I get to a house it is already sold, and the bids are at least 25 percent above the asking price. What should I do?

If you have done your homework, you know exactly what you can afford. If your limit has been reached, just walk away. Do not get caught up in the frenzy. What goes up always, in time, comes down. In the meantime, there can be temporary price declines that create a buyer's market, as we're seeing in parts of the country as I write this, rather than the kind of seller's market we saw in the last half decade.

In almost every bidding war I've seen, the asking price for the house has been significantly under the market value, but it sells way over the market value. Why?

Listing a house under market value is a popular selling technique, especially in hot real estate markets. The point is to get as many people as possible interested in the house; when people see the house, they feel they've found a bargain. Along with lots of other people, they become hooked on the house. That's how a bidding war begins. Before long, the house is sold for much more than the asking price, which was the real estate agent's objective all along.

Real estate prices have been out of sight, but they are starting to come down. This is confusing. I was told that when interest rates fall, the price of homes usually goes up, since homes are more affordable. What is happening?

In late 2000 and early 2001, many investors took a beating in the market. Earlier, people were buying houses based on the size of the paper gains in their stock portfolios or retirement accounts. As they saw that money disappear, they started to curb their spending and decided to hold on to their money instead of buying a house they really didn't need—to wait and see what happened. But because interest rates were also coming down during this debacle, we did not see the decline in prices that we might have expected to see. So you are correct— a decrease in interest rates can tend to hold up the prices of houses even in a declining wealth market.

CONTRACT OF SALE

The contract of sale is a binding agreement between the seller and the buyer. The seller promises to transfer title to his or her property to the buyer at an agreed-upon price. Because the document is binding, it's important to make sure it has all the necessary contingency clauses so that, in case your stated conditions are not met, you can walk away with no liability. The contract must be written, and it should clearly describe all the provisions and conditions of the sale, such as the purchase price, the amount of the down payment, the closing schedule, and whether or not the deal is contingent upon the buyer's obtaining mortgage financing. Other contingencies may include the loan provisions (such as your qualifying for a 30-year fixed-rate loan at no more than 8 percent a year), an acceptable home inspection (usually conducted within 10 to 14 days after the contract is signed), and a termite inspection. Both buyer and seller will sign this document (probably several copies of it), and you should receive an original to keep. Sometimes the contract is referred to as an agreement of sale, contract of purchase, purchase agreement, deposit receipt, or sales agreement. If something in the contract is confusing, don't be afraid to ask for an explanation from your agent or a real estate lawyer. In some parts of the country (e.g., New York City), even if the contract is standard boilerplate, it is customary for an attorney who specializes in real estate to review and explain it.

In some cases, another set of documents, commonly referred to as escrow instructions, will be signed by the seller and the buyer. This agreement includes where the down payment and the deed will be held, the title insurance company, and more. An escrow company is a neutral party that holds the deed, loan documents, and your money until all terms and conditions of the agreement are satisfied.

HOUSE INSPECTIONS

One of the contingencies in your contract of sale will be that the home passes inspection. Now's the time to complete the inspection process, before you make your final purchase.

Inspections—there are often more than one—by a good engineer and/or inspector ensure that the house is sound and without the kinds of problems you can't easily see—termites, structural flaws, geological or environmental risks, or asbestos, to name just a few. Please don't skimp in this area.

I've called around and priced building inspectors. Getting the house inspected will cost me nearly $400. The house is almost brand new. Do you think it's worth the additional expense?

Absolutely. Have you heard the expression, "They don't build them like they used to"? New homes are just as susceptible to faulty construction and other problems as old ones are. Whether you are buying a new home or an old one, please always order an inspection, both for your peace of mind and for the safety of your family and your investment.

MORTGAGES, MORTGAGES, MORTGAGES

If you've followed along this far, you've learned how to create a secure position for yourself as a buyer. You've learned how to establish your purchase price and how to face the real estate market with confidence and minimum emotion. We've discussed the contract of sale. In the following section, we will deal with the mortgage itself: how to shop for one, what to look for, and what to avoid.

USING A MORTGAGE BROKER

Can you explain what a mortgage broker does?

A mortgage broker assists a buyer in finding the best mortgage loan to finance a home. The broker can make the process easier because he or she has access to loan packages from many different lending institutions. A broker can advise you on the maximum loan you can really afford and help you compare mortgages. In addition, he or she will put together and present your entire loan package to the seller or seller's agent, helping you to get through all the needed paperwork and documentation as smoothly and easily as possible.

A good mortgage broker can also advise you about how to handle any minor black marks you may have on your credit history, and may be willing to shave up to half a percentage point off your closing costs by taking a smaller fee.

That said, I strongly recommend that you remain in control of selecting and applying for your mortgage—you need to work *with* a broker, not close your eyes and let the broker do it all.

Isn't it expensive to use a mortgage broker?

Mortgage brokers typically charge you a small fee and also receive a commission from the bank that issues your mortgage. Still, using a broker could save you money if he or she gets you a better mortgage interest rate than you could get on your own.

Does the buyer always pay the mortgage broker's fee?
Normally, the buyer pays the fee. Before deciding to go with a broker, ask him or her to state in writing exactly how much his or her services will cost and who will pay for them.

We didn't go through the preapproval process, so we haven't established a relationship with any particular bank. The seller has accepted our bid, and we have signed the contract of sale. Now the real estate agent says we need to get a mortgage broker and has recommended someone she knows. Should I trust her?
The real estate agent's interest is, of course, in seeing the deal completed as quickly as possible. That said, I wouldn't automatically discount her advice. In fact, you can probably assume that the broker she recommends has had success in getting loans for other clients. Nonetheless, it's important for you to do your homework. Ask your friends for suggestions, meet with other brokers as well as this one, and don't let the agent (or anyone else) pressure you into working with a person with whom you're not comfortable.

Is negotiating directly with a bank a complete waste of time?
No. At the very least, you should check current interest rates charged by the banks in your area. To find a list of current rates at local banks, look in the real estate section of your local paper—rates are usually posted in the Sunday edition. Since rates can change quickly, you may also want to check the Web every day or two. Try *www.bankrate.com.*

From beginning to end, how long does it take to be approved for a mortgage?
As a general rule, the process takes less than three weeks. If

you find it's taking longer, call your broker or lending institution and ask for an explanation for the delay. Don't be shy—remember that you're in control of your money.

I have a great mortgage broker. Why is it important that I learn about the mortgage process? Isn't it a waste of the broker's expertise?

This is a common and unfortunate misconception. Think of a mortgage broker as a guide through the process, not as someone who makes decisions for you. Just as you need to determine your own spending limits, you need to understand the terms of your mortgage—it's a matter of personal power.

FINDING A MORTGAGE ON THE INTERNET

My friend skipped the banker and the broker and is using an Internet service to get a mortgage. What do you think about Internet mortgage services?

The Internet can be a great source of information about interest rates and available mortgages, and can also provide one of the quickest ways to get a loan. But be warned that it can spread misinformation. Some of the most reliable loan sites are *www.lendingtree.com*, *www.quickenloans.com*, and *www.eloan.com*.

LOCKING IN YOUR RATE

What does it mean to lock in an interest rate, and is it a good idea to do it early?

Locking in an interest rate simply means that you have a commitment from a lender for a particular interest rate for a specific period of time: say, a 6 percent rate on a 30-year mortgage, assuming that you close within 60 days. You would lock in the number of points, if any, at the same time. Normally, you are applying for a mortgage on a specific property when you lock in the interest rate.

The longer you have a particular interest rate locked in, the higher the interest rate tends to be, because the bank wants to hedge against interest rates increasing during the longer period of time.

If you think interest rates are going to rise before you close on the property you want to buy, then locking in an interest rate early is an important move. On the other hand, if interest rates are high and expected to go down before you close on your house, try to wait until late in the process to lock in your rate. If you are considering locking in an interest rate, carefully evaluate the terms of the loan, including whether you will have to pay an additional fee in order to lock in.

What happens if I don't lock in an interest rate?

Sooner or later you *will* lock in an interest rate, but in the meantime you will have a floating interest rate. This means that between the time you are approved for a mortgage and the time you close on your home (usually a few months), the interest rate on your loan will float up or down, depending on the going rates. This is something of a gamble and may create some additional anxiety for you if you are worried about rates going up. On the other hand, if you think rates are headed down, it may not be a bad choice.

Why is it that when the Fed lowers interest rates, it does not affect the interest rate of my mortgage?

Fed fund rates only deal with interest in short-term loans. Mortgages are long-term loans, and their fate is determined by what happens with ten-year bonds. When people sell bonds, the price of the bond goes down and therefore interest rates attached to that bond go up. That is why when Alan Greenspan lowered interest rates in June 2003, mortgage rates started to go up the following day. There is no direct correlation with the Fed lowering interest rates and the interest rate of your mortgage; they have nothing to do with each other and never will.

I've heard of a traveling rate lock. What is that?

A traveling rate lock is a locked-in rate you have negotiated before you find a particular house you want to purchase. The rate "travels" with you for a certain period of time (usually 30 to 90 days) as you look at homes. If you think interest rates are going to rise between the time you go shopping for a home and the time you find a place to buy and close on it, you may want to look into a traveling interest rate. Some people suggest that a traveling rate lock is also desirable when you are in a very competitive "seller's market," where you are a stronger candidate as a buyer if you have a mortgage commitment in place.

What happens if I find a property I want to buy during the lock-in period but don't close during that time?

If you do not close on a property in the agreed-upon time period, you will lose the lock-in rate. Deposits and contracts are not enough to sustain a lock-in—you must close the sale. If you paid a fee for the lock-in rate that you didn't use, not closing in time could cost you money. And if interest rates have risen, you could wind up paying more for your mortgage. You should always know for what period your rate is locked in, and keep track of how long you have left before the lock-in expires. Also remember that if you have to postpone your closing, your loan documents will have to be revised and the lender will charge you a fee for the revision—possibly a couple of hundred dollars.

I recently applied for a loan and locked in my rate; however the loan did not close on time and now the bank is not honoring the lock, and the new rate is a lot higher. Can they do that?

Yes, they can, and in fact this actually is exactly what started to happen to many people in July of 2003. Mortgage rates had been going down and down, causing an influx of refinances as well as new home buys. When interest rates started to go back up, everyone was locking in. The problem was that the mortgage companies could not process all the loan requests that they were getting and they were having trouble meeting the closing deadlines. When this happens, some may then say they do not have to honor the lock. So even though you had all your paperwork in, they did not meet the lock deadline. *Trouble.* However, what you need to know is that locks can be extended and it is usually your mortgage broker's responsibility to do this. If you are not working with a mortgage broker, you can do this on your own. Now, this most likely will cost you a small amount of money, but it can be worth it. Also, when applying for a loan in times like this, it is important to stay on top of things and make sure that your lender closes on time, and good mortgage brokers may even offer to take that extra cost to lock out of their own pocket. So when you lock, you have got to stay on top of it big time to see if rates go up after the point of the lock.

Annual Percentage Rate (APR)

When I applied for a loan, the mortgage broker quoted two different rates. One is the annual rate and the other is the APR. What is the APR?

APR stands for annual percentage rate. With some mortgages, your lender will include your closing costs in the amount you are borrowing. The APR is the actual annual rate you will end up paying over the life of the loan, including all additional costs. The annual rate is how much you will be paying per year on the mortgage alone.

Should I make my decision about which mortgage is right for me based on APR?

It's best to compare mortgages based on annual interest rates, not APR. In many instances, comparing based on APR can cost you. In fact, it is a very poor way to comparison shop for a mortgage—and it can easily cause you to make costly wrong decisions.

APR was created in order to provide a way for borrowers to account for additional costs—such as points and fees—that are often associated with a mortgage. This sounds good, because sometimes it isn't easy to choose between a loan with a lower rate and higher fees, say, or a loan with a higher rate and lower fees.

The problem is, the APR calculation makes three very bad assumptions. First, it assumes zero inflation over the years—in other words, that the buying power of a dollar 10, 20, even 30 years from now will be exactly the same as the buying power of a dollar today. Second, the APR calculation assumes that your mortgage will never be paid off, and will certainly not be pre-paid, which means it doesn't take into account the likelihood that you will refinance or sell your home—a major oversight given that the average life of a home mortgage these days is fewer than four years. Finally, APR does not take tax consequences into consideration. This can be significant, since higher fees on a mortgage may not be deductible, while the higher interest rate typically is.

Here is an example of how making a decision based on APR could hurt you if you were considering two loan packages on a

$200,000 fixed-rate 30-year mortgage with zero points. Let's say that Lender A is offering a great low rate of 5.875 percent, and Lender B is offering a higher rate of 6.125 percent. But a closer look shows that Lender A is also charging $3,000 more in fees than Lender B. How do you compare? If you look at APR, Lender A (the one offering 5.875 percent, with $3,000 higher fees) has an APR of 6.1 percent. Lender B (the one with 6.125 but no fees) has an APR of 6.2 percent. So, according to the APR, Lender A is a better deal, even though the fees are $3,000 higher.

This is exactly what all high-fee lenders are hoping you look at—and that you then stop looking and sign right up. But let's look at the real story. Based on the interest rate alone, the payment difference between Mortgage A and Mortgage B is $32 per month. Is it worth paying $3,000 in fees to Lender A in order to save $32 a month? Hardly. It will take you about 8 years just to get your investment back, which makes it an especially bad choice if you think you might move or refinance before then, as most people do.

To make the decision to go with Lender A even worse, if that's possible, borrowers rarely take the value of today's dollars into account. Rather than giving Lender A the windfall of your hard-earned $3,000, you should give it to yourself. Reduce the loan balance on your mortgage by the fees you are saving. In the example above, that would reduce the loan from $200,000 to $197,000—which makes the payment difference based on interest rate just $14 per month, instead of $32 per month! The actual break-even point with Lender A is after 155 months (more than 12 years!).

One more thing: You have to calculate your tax savings on the slightly higher interest rate. When you look at this, it makes even more sense to avoid paying higher, nondeductible fees.

The obvious correct choice is to go with Lender B, even though Lender A has the lower APR.

Bottom line: Forget APR and always, always think twice about advertised low rates when they are accompanied by higher fees.

CONFORMING AND NONCONFORMING LOANS

I'm applying for a loan, and the lender wants to know if I want a conforming loan or a nonconforming loan. What is the difference?

The amount of the loan determines whether it is a conforming loan or a nonconforming loan. Loans under $417,000 are known as conforming loans. Loans above that amount are called nonconforming loans, or jumbo loans. Conforming loans get a better interest rate than nonconforming loans, usually by about one-quarter to one-half of a percentage point. Please note: With the increase in real estate prices over the years, the amount that determines a conforming loan has gone up and up. If you are taking a mortgage or refinancing, check the current ceiling; you may qualify for a lower-rate conforming loan.

Last year, when I got a mortgage, a conforming loan was limited to $359,650. My loan was for $389,650, so it was considered a nonconforming loan and I had to pay a higher interest rate. This year my mortgage amount is considered a conforming loan. What should I do?

In theory, and if the numbers make sense, here's what you should do: If you are planning to stay in this house for as many years as it would take to recoup the costs of refinancing, and the conforming-loan interest rate is low enough to make sense, look into refinancing. Be careful, though, for you may have taken out your original loan at a time when overall interest rates were lower than they are now. Just because your loan now qualifies for a conforming-loan status does not mean the current interest rate environment makes it beneficial to refinance.

PRIVATE MORTGAGE INSURANCE (PMI)

I've tapped into all my resources but I'm just not going to clear the 20 percent down-payment hurdle. I understand I still might be able to get a mortgage, but I will also have to get PMI. Can you explain PMI?

Private mortgage insurance, or PMI, exists for the benefit of banks and lenders. They require that borrowers take out this insurance if they can't put at least 20 percent down on the purchase of a house. Above and beyond the lender's right to foreclose on a house, PMI gives the lender additional protection in case of default. Paying for PMI means that your up-front and monthly expenses will both be larger, although some lenders may offer alternative payment options. PMI doesn't protect you, the borrower. It's meant to protect the lender.

How long will I have to pay PMI?

You usually are required to pay PMI until you have built up at least 20 percent to 22 percent equity in your house. Your equity is based on the fair market value of the property minus the remaining principal amount of your loan. So if you have a home that is worth $200,000 and you owe $190,000 on your mortgage, you have $10,000, or 5 percent, of equity in your home.

How much does PMI cost?

The cost of PMI varies according to the size of the down payment you make (the smaller the down payment as a percentage of the home price, the higher the cost). But if your down payment is 10 percent, say, then PMI will cost you $43 a month for every $100,000 you borrow. Typically, your PMI premium is paid separately from your mortgage, though also on a monthly basis and sent in with your mortgage payment. It is not tax deductible.

To show you how PMI works, let's say you are buying a $200,000 home and making a 10 percent down payment, so you are taking out a $180,000 mortgage. Let's further say it's a 30-year fixed-rate mortgage with a 6 percent interest rate, giving you a monthly mortgage payment of $1,199. Your PMI premium would be $77 a month, on top of your $1,199 monthly mortgage, for a total monthly payment of $1,276. Now, remember, that $77 a month isn't tax-deductible.

Is there a better way to pay my PMI—one that makes it tax-deductible?

Yes, there is. It is called *up-front single premium mortgage insurance*. Here's how it works.

When applying for a mortgage, you can ask your lender to draw up the mortgage so that it lets you pay all your PMI costs up front, as a one-time fee. If you do this with a $180,000, 30-year mortgage, for example, the PMI will add a total of two points, or 2 percent, to the amount of your mortgage, for an additional $3,600 up front. The good news about this is twofold: First, you can add the cost of PMI into your mortgage, so that, rather than forking over the $3,600 in cold, hard cash, you can take out a $183,600 mortgage ($180,000 + $3,600 = $183,600). In this example, when you add your PMI cost to your mortgage, you increase your monthly mortgage payment to $1,224—$24 a month more than the original mortgage—but you also eliminate the $77 monthly PMI fee. So, all told, you save $53 per month. The second part of the good news is that, since PMI is now included in your mortgage, it is tax-deductible, reducing your net after-tax cost even further. *Voila!*

Not bad, right? But here's an even better idea, if you can afford it: Opt for a 25-year mortgage with the PMI paid up front. Because the mortgage has a shorter term, the PMI insurance is going to cost you less—only three-quarters of 1 percent of your loan amount instead of 2 percent. In the example above, the $3,600 up-front cost will be cut to $1,350. Thus, your total loan amount is now $181,350, and your monthly mortgage cost is $1,211—only $11 more a month than the 30-year loan without any PMI! Remember, that's for a 25-year, not a 30-year, term. You will save thousands of dollars in interest payments as a result of the shorter loan term (see page 68), will build equity faster, and can deduct your PMI from your taxes. Smart move!

If I opt for regular monthly PMI payments, will they stop automatically when I've attained 20 percent equity in my home?

Under federal law, PMI on loans made after July 29, 1999, will end automatically once the mortgage is paid down to 78 percent. Each year your lender must send you a reminder that you have PMI and that you have the right to request cancellation if you have met certain requirements.

Even though by law the lender must notify you when your equity has reached the necessary level, this does not always happen. Please make sure that at your closing your lender lets you know in writing under what conditions your PMI costs will be cancelled, and then keep checking; you would be amazed at how a lender can conveniently forget to check on your behalf. For those of you who purchased a home and have a mortgage with PMI before 1999, check your equity level on your own.

Does this law apply to me if I am paying PMI on an FHA loan or on a piggyback or 80/10/10 loan?
No, it does not. Sorry.

I have a high-risk mortgage because I had a terrible credit history and it was the only way I could get a loan. Do the rules that apply to the cancellation of PMI on regular mortgages also apply to me?
No—again, I am sorry, but they do not. Your lender will automatically cancel the PMI halfway through the loan.

Do I get any of the PMI money back after I am no longer paying the premiums?
Assuming that you've always made your monthly mortgage payments in a timely way, the answer is yes. Once you've reached the 20-percent-in-equity mark and after a pre-designated period of time, you should receive from the lender any first-year up-front payment that you made at the time of purchase. Please note: During the first few years of making your mortgage payments, it's important to be very careful to get all your payments in on time, not only to avoid late fees but also because any lapse in payments may be used against you by your lender when it comes time to cancel your PMI policy.

What do I need to do to cancel my PMI?
First, you will need an up-to-date appraisal of the house, confirming that you have indeed reached the 20-percent-in-equity mark. The lender will probably want further proof, such as a

comparable market analysis, that the equity mark is stable (in other words, that the property will hold its value or appreciate). If this is your first home, be aware that the lender may try to reject your claim on the basis of your first-time-buyer status. Or the lender may argue that it expects rapid price fluctuations. So make sure that you are coming to this negotiation armed with a clean credit record and with proof that you have indeed reached the 20-percent-in-equity mark.

I received a big bonus at work and was able to pay ahead enough on my mortgage to reach my 20-percent-in-equity mark in only a year's time. But my bank says I have to pay PMI for at least two years. Is that true?

Some PMI agreements require the borrower to make PMI payments for a predetermined time period. When you are shopping around for your loan, look for an agreement without this clause. If you somehow got stuck with it and find yourself capable of paying ahead more quickly than you thought you could before the required PMI period is up, run the numbers to see whether it makes sense to pay up earlier anyway. You may find that it does, even though you are making some unnecessary PMI payments.

I was told that the best way to get around PMI is to take out what is called an 80/10/10 loan. Can you tell me what that is?

An 80/10/10 loan, also known as a piggyback loan, is becoming a very popular way to get around PMI costs. Remember, any loan for more than 80 percent of the purchase price requires PMI insurance. Let's say you have only 10 percent to put down. Rather than taking out one loan for 90 percent that would require PMI, you take out two loans: one for 80 percent, which does not require PMI, and a second one, often from the same lender, for 10 percent. The 80 percent loan will be at the going interest rate, and the 10 percent loan at a higher rate, in some cases considerably higher. This strategy does enable you to avoid paying PMI on the larger amount; however, it is only wise to do this if you plan to pay off that smaller loan within the next few years.

THE MORTGAGE MENU

There are so many different kinds of mortgages avail-able—I find it very confusing. Can you explain the differences?

There are indeed a lot of different kinds of mortgages, but the main ones among which you will probably be choosing are fixed-rate mortgages, adjustable-rate mortgages, fixed and variable combined mortgages, and Federal Housing Administration (FHA) mortgages. In addition, some mortgages have prepayment penalties if you repay the mortgage before a specific date. Some are due in full when you sell, and others may be taken over by buyers.

Can you explain the interest aspect of a mortgage?

As with any loan, interest on a mortgage is a fee the lender charges for the use of its funds. The cost to you of borrowing the money is the interest rate, which is expressed as a percentage paid annually on the loan. To figure out how much interest you will be paying over the life of your fixed-rate mortgage, deduct the principal amount you are borrowing (say, $200,000) from the total amount you will have to pay back over the life of the loan. Assuming a 6 percent interest rate on a 30-year fixed-rate mortgage, for example, the total amount you must pay over the life of the loan is approximately $431,676. Now subtract $200,000 from $431,676 to calculate the interest you will pay over 30 years on such a loan: $231,676.

Why do I need to know the total amount of interest I'll be paying?

There are two reasons it's helpful to know the total amount of interest you'll be paying. First, it gives you the true cost of owning your home (if you own it until the loan is paid off). Second, it gives you an idea of how much you'll be able to save in taxes over the years, depending on your income-tax bracket. Knowing the total amount of interest you'll pay is one of the benefits of a fixed-rate mortgage.

Is there a way to lower the mortgage interest rate I'll have to pay?

The key to getting the lowest possible interest rate on your mortgage (as well as on your credit cards, car loans, and other consumer credit, by the way) is to make sure you fall within the highest range of FICO scores. FICO scores are a mathematical tool named for the Fair Isaac Corporation, which created them, and are now the single most commonly used criteria for evaluating your creditworthiness when you apply for a loan or a line of credit. (For a full explanation of FICO scores, for information on how to get your score, and for tips on how to improve a score, please see *Ask Suze . . . About Debt.*)

FICO scores range from 300 to 850, and they are divided into ranges that correspond to the interest rates major lenders currently charge. On October 10, 2006, the ranges were:

760–850
700–759
660–699
620–659
580–619
500–579

A score between 300 and 620 puts you in the "sub lenders" category, where it is almost impossible to get a mortgage loan.

To be eligible for the lowest mortgage interest rate, you need to have a FICO score that is in the top range (760–850). If your FICO score is in this range, then you should be aware that technically you qualify to get the best (the lowest) interest rates available. If you are below 620, you are (in your lender's mind) in financial trouble and you will be hit with a seriously high interest rate.

To find the best interest rates available on mortgages, log on to *www.bankrate.com* or *www.lendingtree.com*.

FIXED-RATE MORTGAGES

Fixed-rate mortgages are one of the most popular types available. They are very stable, because the interest rate paid on them is fixed. This means that your monthly payments will always be the same. For example, if you borrow $200,000 at a 6 percent fixed rate for 30 years, the monthly payment will be fixed at $1,199 a month for 30 years.

Can you only get a fixed-rate mortgage for 30 years?
No. A 30-year fixed-rate mortgage was the mortgage of choice for many years, but now you can get a fixed-rate mortgage for different lengths of time, including 10, 15, and 20 years.

Is there an advantage to borrowing for one period of time instead of another?

What is advantageous for you depends on your financial situation. I'll say more about the length of your mortgage later, but basically, there are two rules to keep in mind.

The first rule is that the longer your mortgage term, the higher your interest rate will probably be. In other words, the bank will charge you a higher rate for a 30-year mortgage than for a 15-year mortgage, usually about a quarter- to a half-percent.

The second is that the longer your mortgage term, the lower your payments will be each month. In other words, the monthly payments on a $200,000 mortgage at 6 percent will be $1,199 on a 30-year mortgage, $1,433 on a 20-year mortgage, $1,687 on a 15-year mortgage, and $2,220 on a 10-year mortgage.

How do I know if a fixed-rate mortgage is right for me?

The best time to use a fixed-rate mortgage is when interest rates are low and you think they will be going up, *and* you will be living in the house you want to buy for at least five to seven years. Fixed-rate mortgages are also a good bet if interest rates are low and you are retired or about to retire. If you are living on a fixed income, you'll want to be sure that as many of your expenses as possible, including your mortgage payment, are fixed as well.

ADJUSTABLE-RATE MORTGAGE (ARM)

As you might guess from the name, this type of loan is the opposite of a fixed-rate mortgage. It has an interest rate that falls or rises as general market interest rates fall or rise. Normally, an adjustable-rate mortgage starts with a relatively low interest rate, which is fixed for six months to several years, and then the rate adjusts to market rates. Keep in mind that, in most cases, sooner or later the interest rate on an adjustable-rate mortgage will rise. You may see this type of mortgage referred to as an ARM or a variable mortgage.

Is there any protection for me if I have an ARM and interest rates go sky-high?

Protection should be built into your mortgage agreement in the form of a yearly cap and a lifetime ceiling cap. The yearly cap means that no matter how high interest rates rise, the bank/lender will not be allowed to increase your mortgage rate by more than a specified amount each year, usually about 2 percent. The lifetime ceiling cap means that the interest rate on your mortgage can never exceed a particular figure, usually about 6 or 7 percent more than the original interest rate.

Similarly, if interest rates were to drop significantly, there would be a floor below which the bank wouldn't be obliged to lower your interest rate.

Can you give me an example of how an ARM works?

Say you have a three-year ARM that starts at 4 percent and has a 2 percent yearly cap, a 10 percent lifetime cap, and a minimum interest rate of 3.5 percent. During the first three years of your loan, your interest rate will be fixed at 4 percent. In the fourth year, no matter what interest rates are, the most you will have to pay is 6 percent (4 percent plus the 2 percent annual cap); and the least you will pay is 3.5 percent (because your rate can't drop below that figure). In the following years, the worst that could happen would be that the bank would raise your interest rate by another 2 percent a year—say, from 6 to 8 percent—until the interest rate on your loan reaches 10 percent. Even if interest rates go to 15 or 20 percent, your interest rate will remain at 10 percent.

Obviously, if you are going to take out an adjustable-rate mortgage, you should try to get the lowest possible yearly and lifetime cap, which is more important than either the starting interest rate or the frequency with which your rate can be adjusted.

How often can my interest rate be adjusted?

Many people considering an ARM focus on getting a low starting interest rate and overlook the important issue of the frequency with which their rate can be adjusted. I believe caps and frequency are both more important issues than the starter rate. The interval at which your lender can adjust your rate will be stated in the terms of your loan, and it will probably be either once a year or every six months. As you might imagine, there can be a big difference between the two.

If interest rates are going to rise, an ARM with a lower starting interest rate that can be adjusted every six months could end up costing more than an ARM with a higher starting rate that can be adjusted only once a year. So even if you are going to be stretched during the first few years and are concerned about keeping that starting rate down, I ask you to think long term and consider what might happen after the starter period is over.

Is a rate that changes annually always preferable to one that changes every six months?

If interest rates are low and expected to rise, you will want to lock in the longest possible period between rate changes, which is typically a year. If interest rates are high and expected to fall, you might want to opt for more frequent interest rate adjustments; that way, you benefit more quickly from any rate decreases.

How is the annual increase on an ARM calculated?

Here's how it works: Your interest rate is set on a percentage basis, called a margin, above a designated index. Margins are normally 1 to 5 percent over the selected index. After your starter fixed-rate period ends, the amount by which your lender will be able to increase or decrease the interest rate you pay is based on the rise or fall of the index and the margin of your particular loan. Let's say your mortgage interest rate is tied to the six-month U.S. Treasury bill index and your margin is 2 percent above the index. If the Treasury bill index rises to 6 percent, the maximum your bank could charge you next year would be 8 percent (6 percent plus 2 percent), assuming the increase doesn't exceed your yearly cap amount. When getting an ARM, try to get the lowest possible margin over the index.

Besides the six-month Treasury bill index, what other indexes can the annual increase (margin) be tied to?

The margin also can be set in relation to the Federal Cost of Funds index, the 11th District Cost of Funds Index (COFI), the one-year Treasury Constant Maturity Securities, or the London Interbank Offer Rate (the LIBOR index).

Does it matter which index my ARM is tied to?

Yes, it does. Some indexes are more volatile (they move up and/or down more quickly) than others. Your goal is to be tied to the index that will keep you at the lowest average rate over the course of the mortgage. The problem is, you don't know which index will do this. Remember the general rules, though: When interest rates are high and projected to go lower, you want your mortgage to be tied to an index that fluctuates rapidly so you can cash in on those lower interest rates quickly. If interest rates are fairly low at the time that you get your mortgage, you want an index that changes less often so that you can hold on to that low rate as long as possible.

How do I figure out whether an index is volatile?

Look at how the index has performed in the past. For instance, in the late 1990s, when interest rates were low, the best indexes were the stable ones: the six-month Treasury bill index and the one-year Treasury Constant Maturity Securities. As a general rule, if interest rates rise and the index you are tied to lags, you will save money. Conversely, when interest rates are moving down, you want to be tied to a fast-moving index so that your rate will be lowered more quickly. The COFI (Cost of Funds Index) will probably serve you best in an interest rate environment that is headed down.

Who sets the index rate?

The six-month Treasury bill index is set by the federal government according to the rates it pays on Treasury bills. Your lender does not control the index.

A margin rate can't be too low, right?

Actually, wrong. A rate that's too low can cause what's called a negative amortization. This happens when your monthly payments become so small that they fail to cover the full amount of interest due; then the bank adds that interest to the amount of principal you owe. In this scenario, you could end up owing more than the original mortgage amount! Many adjustable-rate mortgages are susceptible to negative amortization. Ask your lender about your loan.

What should I look at when considering an ARM?

Consider the following issues:

- How long will the starting interest rate be in effect?
- What is the yearly cap on the mortgage?
- What is the lifetime cap on the mortgage?

- What is the lowest interest rate the loan can have?
- Which index is the interest rate going to be tied to?
- What margin can the lender charge you, based on the index?
- Once the initial period has ended, how often can the lender adjust the interest rate?
- Does the mortgage have a negative amortization?
- Is there a penalty if you want to prepay your mortgage?
- Can a new buyer take over your loan?

A number of Internet programs can help you run the numbers using different interest rates and other variables. Make sure to figure out the worst-case scenario. A calculator I like is called "What Will My ARM Loan Payment Be?" at *www.mortgage 101.com.*

FIVE TWENTY-FIVE (5/25) OR SEVEN TWENTY-THREE (7/23) MORTGAGES

What is a fixed and variable combined mortgage?
A fixed and variable combined mortgage (also known as a two-step mortgage) mixes aspects of a fixed-rate mortgage and an ARM. You will probably see these referred to as five twenty-fives (5/25) or seven twenty-threes (7/23), and you can get them as *convertible* or *nonconvertible* mortgages.

What is the difference between a convertible and a nonconvertible mortgage?
I consider a *convertible* two-step mortgage to really be a sort of fixed/fixed-rate mortgage. Here, your interest rate is fixed for the first term of the loan; then it's adjusted once, to another fixed rate, for the remaining 25 or 23 years of the

loan. For example, a convertible 5/25 mortgage would have a fixed interest rate for the first 5 years and then would convert to another fixed interest rate for the remaining 25 years.

With a nonconvertible two-step mortgage, your interest rate is fixed for the first term of the loan. After that, the loan converts to an ARM.

Five and 25 add up to 30, and so do 7 and 23. Are these essentially 30-year mortgages?

Yes, these mortgages will be amortized over 30 years. You choose whether your initial interest rate is fixed for five or seven years and whether, for the remaining 25 or 23 years, you will convert to a new fixed rate or a variable rate that is determined at the time of signing up for the mortgage.

Do nonconvertible mortgages that convert to a variable rate then work like a regular ARM?

Yes. After the initial five or seven years, your adjustment will be tied to an index, to which the lender will probably add a margin of between 1 and 3 percent.

How do I know if a fixed and variable mortgage is a good choice for me?

If you do not plan to live in the home you are buying for at least five or seven years, and if interest rates are going up (making a traditional ARM less attractive), a fixed and variable mortgage might make sense for you. That's because the initial interest rate may be quite a bit lower than the rate on a traditional 30-year fixed-rate mortgage, saving you a lot of money over time. This is something to consider if you are buying a starter home or are pretty sure that you will want to move again soon.

Consider this example. You want a $200,000 mortgage. The interest rate on a 30-year fixed loan will be 6 percent, and the rate on a 5/25 will be 5.5 percent. If you live in the house for the next five years, you will pay $1,199 each month on the fixed loan, for a total of $71,940. With a 5/25 loan, you will pay $1,136 each month, for a total of $68,196. If you sell your house at the end of five years, you will have saved more than $3,744 by having the 5/25.

Is there any difference between the 5/25 and the 7/23, aside from the different periods of time that you keep your initial fixed rate?

Because you are locking in the rate for a longer period with a 7/23, the interest rate may be a quarter- or half-point higher than on a 5/25.

PORTABLE MORTGAGE

I've heard a lot about a new kind of mortgage that I should check out called a portable mortgage. What exactly is a portable mortgage?

A portable mortgage allows a borrower to keep their mortgage if they move to a different primary residence. Portable mortgages had been creating quite a buzz in a favorable-interest-rate environment, but before jumping into a portable mortgage, please compare your options, because in almost all cases a portable mortgage just does not make sense. Here's how they work. Let's say a 30-year fixed rate with zero points is being offered at a rate of 5.875 percent. The remaining balance can be transferred to a new primary residence when the borrower moves. The rate would remain at 5.875 percent, and the loan would continue to amortize without being reset to 30 years.

Does a portable mortgage cost me more than a fixed mortgage?

You are paying a premium of roughly 50 basis points in rate for this type of mortgage, so the longer you remain in the home, the more you stand to lose. If you intend to stay or wind up staying in the home for 10 years or more, this mortgage is a poor choice because you pay a much higher rate for the first 10 years.

If I am only going to be staying in my home for the next five years and not rebuying another house, should I get a portable mortgage or an ARM?

Here is a rule of thumb: If you intend to move within five years, then you would be much better off selecting a 5/1 ARM, where the interest rate is locked for five years and then changes every year after that.

If I plan to sell my house in a short period of time and buy another home, does it make sense to get a portable mortgage?

That depends on what happens to interest rates and how much of a home you plan to buy. Since you can only take the remaining balance with you when you change residences, you may find yourself requiring additional funds to close. This may cause you to need a second mortgage or home equity line of credit in order to make up for the shortfall in funds required to purchase your new home. The second mortgage will likely be at a higher or variable interest rate, thus negating or minimizing the benefit of the portable mortgage.

When does a portable mortgage make sense?

If you are on a fixed income, expect to move within four to

seven years, have very low risk tolerance, expect to downsize during your next move, and think interest rates are going to be higher when you do move, then the portable mortgage may be a good option for you.

FEDERAL HOUSING ADMINISTRATION (FHA) MORTGAGE

As of 2006, the Federal Housing Administration (FHA) offers mortgages ranging from about $200,160 to $362,790 for a single-family home (depending on the region of the country), with as little as 3 percent down. The FHA, a division of the federal government controlled by the Department of Housing and Urban Development (HUD), may be willing to give you a mortgage even if you have had bad credit in the past.

What are the differences between qualifying for an FHA mortgage and for a conventional mortgage?
FHA uses a more relaxed standard to approve you for a loan than a conventional lender would. The FHA specifies that your loan payments should be no more than 31 percent of your gross monthly income. Even so, it is ultimately your responsibility to calculate what you will be able to pay.

What counts as part of my monthly housing costs?
Your monthly housing costs are made up of your mortgage principal, interest, taxes, and insurance—often abbreviated as PITI.

Does the FHA let me have a higher PITI than a conventional lender?
Yes. If your gross monthly income is $3,000 and you are allowed by a conventional lender to have a PITI payment

equal to 28 percent, then you know that you cannot spend more than $840 each month on housing costs ($3,000 multiplied by 0.28 equals $840). A conventional lender will also limit your total debt, including credit cards, to between 33 and 36 percent of your gross monthly income.

The FHA will allow you to have higher debt-to-income ratios. If your PITI can be 31 percent of your gross monthly income, as the FHA allows it to be, multiply $3,000 (your gross monthly income) by 0.31. You can spend up to $930 each month on your PITI. Further, the FHA allows you to have a total long-term debt ratio of up to 43 percent of your gross monthly income.

Are the interest rates offered by the FHA comparable to a conventional loan?

Yes, they are essentially the same.

If I get a mortgage from a regular bank and put less than 20 percent down, I have to pay for PMI. If I get a mortgage from the FHA and put less than 20 percent down, do I still have to get insurance?

Yes. The FHA will issue the insurance, charging you about 1.5 percent (as of 2006) of the loan amount up front, which may be included in closing costs, and about 0.5 percent of the loan amount divided by 12 to be paid monthly.

Is there a maximum FHA loan amount I can apply for?

Yes, though the amount varies by county and can change from year to year. The size of the loan you may be eligible for will depend on the county that you live in and the median price of real estate in your area. Contact your local FHA office, which you can find on the Web at *www.hud.gov/local.index.cfm.*

Who is best served by an FHA mortgage?

If you have had problems with your credit history or have very little money to use as a down payment, and if you want to avoid closing costs, an FHA loan may be your best bet.

When you say that I can have "problems" with my credit history and still get an FHA mortgage, does that include bankruptcy?
Yes. If your bankruptcy was discharged at least two years before you apply for a loan, the FHA will consider your application. No lender, however, including the FHA, will give you a mortgage if you are currently considered a bad credit risk and/or do not have sufficient income to carry a mortgage obligation.

Flex 97 Mortgages

What is a Flex 97 mortgage?
The Flex 97 is a conventional fixed-rate home loan that is designed to assist first-time home buyers of a primary residence. The minimum down payment required for this type of loan is 3 percent of the sales. Funds for the 3 percent can come from one or more of the following sources: gifts from relatives, grants from an employer or nonprofit organization, secured loan from a 401(k) or life insurance policy, or personal savings. In order to qualify, most lenders require a credit score of at least 660. So if you want to take advantage of the low interest rates and have a good credit record but have not been able to accumulate enough money for a down payment and closing costs, this mortgage might be right for you.

Assumable Mortgages

What is an assumable mortgage?
An assumable mortgage allows the buyer to "assume" the seller's current mortgage. If the seller's current mortgage is a

lower rate than current mortgage rates, then this sort of mortgage makes sense. Most mortgage loans have a due-on-sale clause preventing the loan from being assumed by the new owner, although the Federal Housing Administration mortgages and mortgages supplied by the Department of Veterans Affairs can be assumed. It's important to note that assumable loans are rare and only available for the principal balance.

INTEREST ONLY MORTGAGES

What is an interest-only mortgage?

Interest-only mortgages require the borrower to pay interest only for the first few years, and interest and principal in the later years of the loan. This type of loan is popular with individuals who are self-employed with inconsistent incomes or professionals who are just beginning their careers such as lawyers or doctors who know that their incomes will significantly increase in a few years.

BALLOON LOAN

What is balloon loan?

In a fixed loan, the principal and interest have been amortized over the life of the loan. In a balloon loan, only the interest, or some combination of interest and principal, have been paid when the loan term expires. The balance is due in full, which is called a balloon payment. The balloon payment is more common to second mortgages. For example, if you borrow $10,000 for ten years and your monthly payments have included only interest, you must pay the $10,000 in principal at the end of the term. Similar to ARM loans, balloon loans are another option to get a lower interest rate in the first few years of the mortgage. These mortgages charge less interest for a set time frame, but require the borrower to either refinance at the end of that period, pay off the loan, or convert it to a fixed payment schedule. Please be very careful with balloon loans. Since no one can predict how interest rates will increase, you can find yourself in a situation where you have to refinance at a high interest rate, or you may be forced to sell your home to pay the balloon loan.

LOANS FOR VETERANS

What is a VA loan?
VA stands for Veterans Affairs, and a VA loan is a loan or a mortgage that the Department of Veteran Affairs makes available for all those considered to be veterans.

Who is eligible for a VA loan?
Veterans who served on active duty during wartime for 90 days or more; veterans with active service only during peacetime who have served more than 180 days; veterans of enlisted service that began after September 7, 1980, or officers with service beginning after October 16, 1981, who in most cases have served at least two years are all eligible for a VA loan.

If you are full-time active duty military personnel who have served for at least 60 days, you are also eligible for a VA loan, as well as Reservists and National Guard members who served in support of operations in Kosovo, Afghanistan, or Iraq for at least 90 days. Reservists and National Guard members who have completed six years of service and have been honorably discharged or who are still serving may also be eligible.

I am eligible for a VA mortgage. What are the advantages of going this way, or should I just get a conventional mortgage?

VA loans, I think, are really quite attractive, especially when interest rates are low. The reason is that if you sell your house, the VA loan is assumable by the next buyer even if they are not a veteran. The new buyer would have the same terms as your loan.

Another advantage of a VA loan is that given today's high prices of homes in some areas, you might not have saved enough money to put down the required 20 percent to avoid PMI (Private Mortgage Insurance) costs. With a VA loan, even if you do not have 20 percent to put down, in fact even if you have 0 percent to put down, you can still get a loan without having to pay that extra PMI cost.

I heard VA loans are not worth the trouble because the application process takes forever to complete. Is that true?

It used to be true years ago, but that is no longer true today. The Department of Veterans Affairs has made the application process far simpler, and today applying for a VA loan is very similar to applying for a conventional mortgage. Make sure you get a certificate of eligibility, which you can find on the VA website *www.homeloans.va.gov,* or you can call (800) 827-1000 for more information.

With a VA loan how much can I borrow to buy a home if I have no money to put down?

As of the year 2006 you can borrow up to $417,000 to buy or build a home. If you have more than 5 percent to put down, you could get a reduced funding fee.

If I already have a VA loan, can I refinance?

You absolutely can, and the process should not take more than a week.

THE LENGTH OF
THE MORTGAGE

Which is better, a 15-year or a 30-year mortgage?
I will say more about this later, but as a general rule I recommend the 15-year mortgage to those who can afford the higher monthly payments associated with the shorter payment period. Here's why. (Please note that these figures do not take into account any interest tax deduction.) If you borrow $200,000 at 6 percent for 15 years, every month you will pay the lender $1,688. At the end of your mortgage term, you will have paid a total of $303,840. If you borrow $200,000 at 6 percent for 30 years, your monthly payments will be lower—about $1,199—but you'll be making those payments for twice as long. After 30 years, you will have paid a grand total of $431,640. Once you do the math, it becomes clear that a 15-year mortgage can save you money—in this example, $127,800.

Can you explain in more detail the difference between a 15-year and a 30-year mortgage?
Before I explain this, I want to remind you that there are also 10-year, 20-year, and even 40-year mortgages. But 15- and 30-year mortgages are the most popular ones by far.

The basic difference between a 15- and a 30-year mortgage is obviously the length of the loan. Beyond that, the interest rate on a 15-year mortgage is typically half a percent lower than on a 30-year mortgage; as a tradeoff, you will pay a larger sum each month. For a long time, 30-year mortgages were the standard (and sometimes the only) choice for most people,

COMPARING MONTHLY PAYMENTS ON MORTGAGES
OF DIFFERENT TERMS

MORTGAGE AMOUNT	MONTHLY PAYMENTS 15 YEARS 5.5%	30 YEARS 6%	PER-MONTH DIFFERENCE	TOTAL INTEREST SAVINGS WITH 15-YEAR VS. 30-YEAR LOAN
$50,000	409	300	109	$34,400
$100,000	817	600	217	$68,700
$150,000	1,226	899	327	$103,000
$200,000	1,634	1,119	435	$137,500
$250,000	2,043	1,499	544	$171,900
$300,000	2,451	1,799	652	$206,300
$400,000	3,268	2,398	870	$275,100
$500,000	4,085	2,998	1,087	$343,800

which is why many of us still think of them as the way to go. But it pays to do the math.

I bought my own first house by taking out a 30-year mortgage. I didn't know I had a choice, and I was told, "Oh, everyone gets a 30-year mortgage," so that's what I did. Almost ten years later, I realized that the difference per month would have been only about $115. If I had realized that I could own my home in 15 years instead of 30 for an extra $115 each month, you can bet I would have figured out a way to come up with the extra money. In many places, the difference between the payment on a 15-year mortgage and on a 30-year mortgage will usually not be more than $400 a month.

Another benefit of a shorter term: If you are not inclined to put your monthly savings from the smaller payments on a 30-year mortgage into an investment account for your future, the higher payments on a 15-year mortgage will effectively do your saving for you.

How large are the savings on a 15-year mortgage, compared with a 30-year mortgage?

The table on page 68 demonstrates the differences between the shorter and longer mortgage term, both in monthly payments and in overall costs, based on common loan amounts. This table assumes that you'll keep the house for the full life of the loan and does not take into account your tax deductions for interest payments.

Note: Please keep in mind that if you borrow more than a specific sum (in the year 2006, about $417,000), your mortgage will be considered a jumbo loan, which usually commands an interest rate half a percent higher than a smaller loan amount would. Thus, interest rates for a jumbo loan in the example above will be 6 percent on a 15-year mortgage and 6.5 percent on a 30-year mortgage.

Why don't more people get 15-year mortgages?

I think that when we consider what we can afford at the time that we buy our homes, we try to stay safe. We figure that as we earn more money, we can pay off our mortgage faster. But few of us are disciplined enough to pay more money than is required, even as our incomes rise.

Look at it this way: If you make payments on a 7 percent, 30-year mortgage, after 15 years of making payments you will still owe almost 75 percent of your original balance. If you take a 15-year mortgage, you will own your home outright at that time.

Why is the tax deduction on a mortgage so much larger at the beginning of the loan?

Because loans are structured so that you are paying mostly interest for the first few years. And the interest payments are the part that is tax-deductible.

Here's how a typical loan is structured:

During the first year of a 30-year loan, only 13 percent of your monthly payments goes toward paying off the principal amount you borrowed, and 87 percent goes toward paying off the interest.

By the 10th year of the loan, 25 percent of your payment goes to paying off the principal and 75 percent goes to paying interest.

By the 20th year, 50 percent of your payment is applied to the principal and 50 percent goes to paying interest.

By the 25th year, 70 percent of your payment will go to principal and 30 percent will go to interest.

By the 30th and final year, 99.5 percent of your payment will be applied to principal and only 0.5 percent will go to interest. That's not much of a tax deduction for you—but you'll still be paying the same monthly sum.

POINTS

What are points?

A point is the equivalent of 1 percent of the total amount of the mortgage. A lender generally charges points up front for lending you money. The lender usually also dictates the number of points you pay, but this is typically a negotiable issue. Expect to pay fewer, or no, points with a higher-interest-rate loan and more points with a lower-interest-rate loan.

Do I have to pay the points before I start to make payments on my mortgage?

Typically, yes. Points are due in cash at the time of the closing (when the seller transfers the house to you). Sometimes the lender will let you add the cost of the points to the amount of your mortgage, in which case you will pay them off over time. Please be careful here; in essence, you'll be paying interest on the points.

My lender is offering me a lower interest rate if I pay a certain number of points up front. How does this work, and is it a good idea?

It's very common for a lender to offer you a range of combinations of points and interest rates. For example, a bank might offer you an interest rate of 7 percent and no points, or an interest rate of 6.8 percent and one point, or an interest rate of 6.5 percent and two points, and so on. Different lenders will offer different combinations. You also can "buy down" your mortgage by paying more up front in points to get an even lower interest rate. For example, you might offer to pay four points in exchange for an interest rate of 5 percent.

Lenders have a lot of flexibility in setting points, so feel free to negotiate. But watch out when your mortgage is an ARM; since the initial rate may be in effect for only a year or two, paying a big chunk of money to buy down the initial rate could harm rather than help you. And in every case, take into consideration how long you plan to stay in the house; the shorter your stay, the less sense paying points up front may make.

My real estate agent says that paying points is a good idea because they are tax-deductible. Is that true?

Points paid as prepaid interest that meet IRS tests are tax-deductible in the year that you close. Whether paying them is a good idea really depends on the answers to two questions: Again, how long are you planning to live in the house? And what will the difference in your monthly payments be? Once you've answered these questions, it's time to crunch some numbers.

Say you want to borrow $200,000 for 15 years, and a bank is willing to lend it to you at an interest rate of 6.8 percent and no points, or at 6.5 percent and one point, or at 6.25 percent and two points. First, figure out how much each option will cost you up front, at the closing. Of course, you'd owe nothing if you have no points to pay. You'd owe $2,000 if you have to pay one point ($200,000 multiplied by 0.01), and $4,000 if you have to pay two points.

Next, compare your monthly payments. If you borrow $200,000 for 15 years at 6.8 percent, you will have to pay $1,775 each month, or $319,500 over the life of the loan. If you borrow $200,000 for 15 years at 6.5 percent, you will pay $1,743 each month, or $313,740 over the life of the loan. If you borrow $200,000 for 15 years at 6.25 percent, you will pay $1,715 each month, or $308,700 over the life of the loan.

Finally, add the cost of the points to your total payment in each scenario. In the first situation, you pay no points, so $319,500 is the total amount this mortgage would cost you. In the second situation, add $313,740 to the $2,000 you will pay in points: This mortgage would cost a total of $315,740. In the last situation, you would pay $4,000 in points, so add $4,000 to $308,700: This mortgage would cost you $312,700.

This is just a simple calculation to give you a sense of what to look for. But think about this: If you paid just one point on this loan, or $2,000, versus two points, or $4,000, what would that $2,000 be worth if you invested it over the life of the loan? If you consider the question this way, you will really know if it is worth paying those points. Just so you know, after 15 years at an 8 percent annual rate of return, $2,000 would be worth $6,344 before taxes. After taxes you would probably come out almost even. In real life, the chances of your investing that money over that period of time are almost nil. But as you can see, there are many ways to look at this, and what you choose to do will depend on your particular situation. Get professional help to make sure you have taken everything into consideration.

What else should I take into consideration before deciding to pay points up front?

Before you decide that the two-point, 6.25 percent interest rate combination is the way to go, remember the two questions I told you to ask yourself. You've answered the question about monthly payments: With this option, they will be reduced. As to the second question: If you think that you will really stay in the house you are purchasing for the full 15-year term of the mortgage, then, yes, it is probably worth paying the extra money in points in order to get the lower interest rate. (Studies show, however, that the average family buys and sells every five to seven years.) We didn't even calculate the tax savings you would get in the year that you paid the points in cash, which, assuming you are in the 28 percent tax bracket and you paid $4,000, would be $1,120. But, as you can see, the tax savings alone should not be the determining factor when deciding how many points to pay on your mortgage.

What if I have to finance the points?

That complicates the question, because the objective of paying the points is to lower your interest rate and save money over the life of the loan. If you finance the points, you'll be *increasing* the size of your debt by the value of the points and, of course, you will be paying interest on the additional money you borrowed, too. Try not to do it.

ESCROW ACCOUNTS

My lender wants me to add my property taxes and home insurance to my mortgage payments every month, for deposit in an escrow account. Is this a good idea?

No. In fact, if you have a choice in the matter, I would run in the opposite direction. Many lenders require these payments to be made with your mortgage, but many others do not, though by law they have the right to do so. Here's how they work. You pay the lender monthly, and the lender holds the money in an escrow account or in trust on your behalf, and then pays the taxes and insurance for you. At least, that's the way it is supposed to work. The kicker is that sometimes the lenders themselves do not make the payments. I have known quite a few people who have received notice from their insurance companies that their policies have lapsed. Another kicker is that in the majority of states, lenders do not have to pay you interest on the money they are holding for you.

In which states do lenders have to pay interest on escrow accounts?

Fourteen states require the payment of interest on escrow accounts: California, Connecticut, Iowa, Maine, Maryland, Massachusetts, Minnesota, New Hampshire, New York, Oregon, Rhode Island, Utah, Wisconsin, and Vermont.

If I have a mortgage that requires an escrow account, do I have to pay into it forever?

Generally, escrow payments are required for the entire term of the loan. However, some lenders might consider a reduction or waiver of the escrow requirement once a certain amount of the loan is paid back. Since this varies from lender to lender, I recommend that you discuss this with your prospective lender and/or mortgage broker.

I am about to get an FHA loan and I have been told that an escrow account is mandatory. Is that true?
No. Escrow accounts are not mandatory on FHA loans, no matter what a lender may say. The issue is at the discretion of the lender. If you are applying for an FHA loan, try to find a lender who will waive the escrow arrangement. If the lender says no, offer instead to set up a savings account with that lender, keeping your tax and insurance money in your own name, earning interest. In fact, in many states if you offer to do this, the lender by state law must waive the escrow requirement. Ask your real estate agent if this is true in your particular state. But please be careful: Many lenders who agree to waive your escrow accounts will then try to charge you a one-time waiving fee of about 1 percent of the loan amount. Ouch.

TITLE INSURANCE

If you're buying a home, you can be sure that the bank that's providing your mortgage will ask you to buy title insurance. Here's what you need to know.

What is title insurance?
Title insurance is insurance coverage that protects your mortgage lender against a mistaken or incomplete title search by a

title company—for example, a search that fails to turn up a lien against the title, such as for back property taxes or a disputed title claim—and promises to pay the costs of settling such claims.

How much will title insurance cost?

It's important for you to know that title insurance protects the bank that approves your mortgage loan, not you, against any title claims. So typically, it covers the amount of a mortgage, and the policy's value declines as the mortgage is paid off. You pay the premium just once—when the loan is taken out. Typical rates are several tenths of a percent of the mortgage amount—often between 0.4 and 0.7 percent. This adds up to between $800 and $1,400 for a $200,000 loan.

Since traditional title insurance only protects the bank, should I buy title insurance that protects me as well?

Yes, probably. It's not a bad idea for you to have this kind of insurance, because the cost is just several hundred dollars more. Without it, you wouldn't be protected at all from a title problem. But if you do buy your own policy, check for exceptions that may leave you with less protection than you want. If any exceptions are a concern, ask the title insurer if they can be taken off the policy.

If I am about to get a second mortgage, do I have to get title insurance for my lender?

Not all lenders require title insurance on a second mortgage, but many who focus on a higher-risk market—large second-mortgage loans or loans turned down by banks but accepted at higher rates by finance companies—do require title insurance. It should cost slightly less that the title coverage on a large first mortgage—perhaps 0.3 or 0.4 percent.

What should I ask for when shopping for title insurance? Is there any way to lower the premium I am about to be charged?

It's possible to lower the cost of title insurance. Try taking the following steps.

- Ask the seller to pay for your coverage. In some states, the seller must pay. In others, it's something that can be negotiated.
- Ask the title insurer or the lawyer doing the new title search whether you can have the seller's title policy reissued to you. If the policy isn't too old and the insurer agrees, you may be able to save hundreds of dollars.
- Shop around. In some states, there have been charges that real estate agents are getting kickbacks from title insurers to send business their way. Honest insurers don't pay kickbacks, of course, and prices vary. Don't be afraid to ask for the best deal.

TAKING TITLE TO YOUR HOME

When you buy a piece of property, the way you take title—that is, the way ownership is recorded on the deed—becomes very important. There are five main variations on how people take title to a house: as an individual, joint tenancy with right of survivorship, tenants in common, tenancy by the entirety, and community property. These opinions are discussed in detail in *Ask Suze . . . About Wills and Trusts*.

It's worth repeating here, however: In almost *all* cases—whether you are an individual, a married couple, or two individuals, and no matter how you choose to hold the property—title to your home should be held in a living trust.

How should married couples take title to a home in states that aren't community-property states?

In states that aren't community-property states, married couples are usually (but not always) best off when they take title to a home by what's known as joint tenancy with right of survivorship (JTWROS). Joint tenancy with right of survivorship means that two or more owners each have equal ownership in the whole property. It is a very efficient way to own property together and be sure that it will change hands after death with minimum complications and expenses. When you hold something in JTWROS and one joint tenant dies, his or her ownership is automatically passed to the remaining joint tenant or tenants without having to go through probate court. In fact, you cannot will or otherwise leave your interest in a property held in joint tenancy to anyone other than your joint tenant or tenants. (JTWROS is not limited to married couples; life partners and others can use it, too.)

An important benefit of taking title this way is that when one joint tenant dies, his or her portion of the property receives what's known as a step up (or down) in cost basis, which is used to calculate taxes owed on any gain in the value of the home. This can represent a tremendous tax savings if the surviving spouse, tenant, or tenants has to sell the house.

Here's what that means: If you and your spouse or life partner buy your house for $300,000, that $300,000 is considered the cost basis of the property for tax purposes. Since you both own the property equally, the cost basis is shared equally between you, which means that, in essence, you each have a $150,000 cost basis in the house. Let's say that many years later, when your partner dies, your house is worth $650,000.

The new tax basis for this property will now be half the value of the house at the time that your partner dies, in this example, $325,000, plus your original cost basis of $150,000, or $475,000. The step up in tax basis on your deceased spouse's or partner's half of the property represents a tremendous tax savings to you because it reduces the amount of money you could be liable to pay in capital-gains tax if you sold the house.

If you want to leave your share of your home to someone other than your spouse, however, joint tenancy with right of survivorship is *not* the way to go.

What's the best way for married couples to take title in a community-property state?

The best way to take title is by community property. Community property is defined as any property and income accumulated by and belonging jointly to a married couple. Taking title this way is similar to taking title by joint tenancy with right of survivorship, except that community property is available only to married couples and it carries an additional benefit: When one spouse dies, the other spouse gets a step up (or down) in tax basis on the *whole* property, not just half of it. In many cases, this step up confers a huge tax advantage. The only problem is that in most cases transfer is not automatic, so it's advisable for married couples to hold homes held by community property in a revocable living trust or, if your state allows, to hold title in community property with right of survivorship. This means that when one spouse dies, the other spouse automatically owns the property and does not have to go through probate court. This is the best possible way for married couples to take title.

Which states allow property to be held as community property?

Community-property states include Arizona, California, Idaho, Louisiana, Nevada, New Mexico, Texas, Washington, and Wisconsin.

Which states allow title to be taken by community property with right of survivorship?
Arizona, California, Nevada, Texas, and Wisconsin let married couples add the right of survivorship to community property.

I am in my second marriage. Both my new husband and I have children from our previous marriages. We are about to buy a home together, using money we accumulated before we met each other and, although we plan to live in the house for the rest of our lives, we would like our respective children to inherit the money each of us has invested in it if something happens to us. What is the best way to take title?
The best way for you to take title is under a format known as tenants in common, or TIC—*not* by joint tenancy with right of survivorship. Here is the difference. When you take title in JTWROS, when the first spouse dies the house automatically passes to the remaining spouse or joint tenant. This kind of ownership overides the wishes contained in a will or living trust. In other words, no matter what your will says, if you die, the house will pass directly to your husband. If your husband's will or living trust leaves everything *he* owns to his own children, then when he dies his children will inherit your share of the house as well as his. Your children will receive nothing.

When you take title by TIC, this problem disappears. Your will or trust will be the document that dictates who will inherit your portion of the home when you die.

There's a problem with this, too, of course: Your children

(or his, if he dies first) may want to sell their interest in the home, meaning that the remaining spouse might have to buy them out or move. That puts a serious burden on the remaining spouse. To solve that problem, what you could do is to set up a trust, known as a QTIP trust, with the title of the house held in TIC. Upon your death, your half of the house would pass into the QTIP trust, which would allow your husband to keep the house as long as he lives or wants to remain there. When he dies, that half of the house would pass directly to your children.

My husband has severe credit card debt, and I am afraid his creditors will come after our home. I live in a state that allows residents to hold title in tenants by the entirety, and I have been told that this would protect the house from creditors. Is that correct?

Yes, it is. Tenants by the entirety can be a very good way for married couples—but only married couples—to take title to a property, though only about 30 states permit it. In general, it operates much as JTWROS does; each spouse owns the property equally, and when one spouse dies the property passes automatically to the surviving spouse without going through probate. But here is the additional benefit: As long as you own your home by tenancy in the entirety, no creditor can come after the home (or any other asset that you hold this way). The reason: Each tenant is considered separate, so tenants are not liable for each other's debts, and the home is completely protected against creditors. Please know, however, that once you sell the home, you are fair game for creditors who go after the sale money, since that money is no longer protected by tenancy by the entirety. As long as you own your home under this kind of title, however, creditors cannot touch it at all.

I have just received a large inheritance from my father, and I want to use some of the money to buy a home for my wife and me. The problem is that I promised my father I would protect his legacy—that I wouldn't let anything happen to it in case of a divorce. How should I take title to the house?

Keeping a home as a separate asset within a marriage can be tricky. Typically, when a person inherits property or cash and wants to keep it safe from the possibility that a spouse will make a financial claim against it during a messy separation or divorce, the first spouse simply takes care not to commingle this asset or cash with any property belonging to the other spouse or with any property or money held jointly by the couple. You would keep your inherited property in your name only, without allowing your spouse access to it, and that would be that. With a house, however, the question of who makes the mortgage payments, pays the taxes, and pays for home improvements arises; if your wife contributes time or money to any of these, you may find that she has a claim to part of the appreciation in the value of the property in the event of a separation or divorce. Please make sure that you consult a good real estate lawyer or trust attorney to protect the wishes of your father.

CLOSING THE DEAL

Simply put, this is the moment when you are "closing," or completing, the deal. People wonder why there needs to be a formal closing and why they have to pay so many fees for what should be a simple process. There are a lot of reasons for the rules surrounding a closing; most of these rules are meant to protect everyone involved. What would you do if it turned out that the title the seller transferred you was a fake and the money you gave him or her had disappeared?

When you buy or sell a home, everybody wants guarantees—the seller wants a guarantee that the buyer's check is worth more than the paper on which it is written; the buyer wants a guarantee that the title being exchanged for the check is legitimate; the real estate agent wants a guarantee that she will be paid the agreed-upon commission for the sale. The closing protects the bank, the buyer, the seller, the agent, and anyone else involved from fraud. The following section is meant to help you close the deal safely, without jeopardizing your investment.

PRECLOSING INSPECTION

We had the house we're buying inspected by a professional right after our bid was accepted. It's been only a month since then, and we're ready to close. Do we still need to perform a preclosing inspection?

Yes. For one thing, you'll want to make sure that everything you contracted to buy is still in the house at closing time. Let me tell you the story of my friend Ann, who skipped the preclosing inspection. Buying the house had been easy because during the negotiations, the woman Ann was buying from became a friend. As contracts were being signed, Ann and the seller spoke candidly and came to a verbal agreement about what was and wasn't going to be left behind. Most of that conversation was easy and pleasant, but when Ann brought up the antique sconces in the dining room, there was a long pause before the seller told Ann that the sconces were part of the house and would be left behind.

A month later, Ann called this woman to make her preclosing appointment for the day before they were scheduled to sign everything. The seller told Ann that she was swamped with her own move. She asked if Ann could just skip it, saying, "Everything is exactly as you remember it." Ann, who was busy, too, agreed. Sure enough, when Ann walked into the dining room on the day after the closing, everything was exactly as she remembered it—minus the sconces!

Okay, so this wasn't the end of the world. But what if the seller had taken more than just a few light fixtures? What if Ann walked in and found the light fixtures, the refrigerator, and the air conditioners missing?

This happens more often than you might think, so please make the time for a preclosing inspection.

When should I schedule a preclosing inspection?

Try to schedule the inspection for the day before the closing, and make sure to schedule it no earlier than two days beforehand. As soon as you have a closing date, call the real estate agent or the seller to set a date. From this point in the process, you are in the driver's seat. If the seller cannot be present for the inspection, then it's easy enough to get the keys from the agent.

I've scheduled my preclosing inspection. What should my wife and I look for as we walk through the house?

Make sure the home has not sustained any unexpected damage since you signed the contract of sale. Remember, as a buyer, you probably haven't seen the inside of your future home since your bid was accepted, 30 to 60 days ago or more. Things can change in that time. Here's a four-point plan for a successful walk-through:

1. Checklist: List all the items the seller has agreed to leave behind, bring the list with you, and use it. Never rely on a verbal agreement.

2. On and Off: Test everything that can be turned on and off, including the lights, the refrigerator, the water (hot and cold) in the kitchen and bathrooms, the dishwasher, and the washer and dryer. Let the water run for a few minutes so you can make sure that it flows where it is supposed to flow, and keep all the appliances running from the time you enter the house until the time you leave (at least 45 minutes).

3. Open and Close: Quickly open and close all windows and doors, and don't overlook the oven doors, washer and dryer doors, closet doors, and pantry doors. Make sure you can open and close everything without a problem. The other reason to do this is that you never know what surprises you might find in a cellar or a remote closet—this check can reveal holes in the walls, droppings, or other signs of infestation. Obviously, your inspector should have checked for these back when you were signing the contract of sale, but anything can develop, particularly if there has been a lengthy delay before the closing.

4. Broken or Damaged: Ideally, the house should be completely empty when you do the walk-through, so that you can make sure nothing was damaged when the seller moved out. Make sure there is no visible damage to the ceilings, floors, or walls—look for large cracks or water damage; you may be shocked to discover what the seller's furniture or Oriental rugs were hiding. If you are buying a home in a condominium building or a cooperative, it is probably worthwhile to knock on the downstairs neighbor's door and ask if there has been any water damage or leaks recently from your future home. If the house is not yet empty, it may be difficult for you to confirm these things, so

take your time and consider taking photographs of the condition of the house if you are nervous about the seller's movers inflicting damage.

Can I bring somebody to help with the preclosing inspection?

Yes. You can bring anyone you choose to the preclosing inspection. But you should bring only people who can help you evaluate the state of the house you're about to purchase. Unlike your initial inspection, the preclosing inspection is strictly for determining that your house is in the condition you expect. You should have your real estate agent there, and if you're purchasing the house with a partner, both of you should be present. A professional engineer is probably unnecessary.

The sellers are insisting that they need to be present during the inspection, and my realtor says they have a right to be there. What should I do if I find something wrong?

Do absolutely nothing until you've left the house. Do not raise an issue with the sellers directly or, for that matter, with the seller's real estate agent. If you find something damaged, just make a note of it. Let's say you notice a broken windowpane. After you and your own real estate agent have left the premises, tell him or her what the problem is and let the agent address the issue with the seller's agent. If you are not working with your own agent, you will probably want to present the issue to your attorney, who can also deal with either the seller's agent or his or her attorney.

If your seller insists on being present during this inspection, try to avoid answering any questions he or she may have for you. Sometimes a seller will make informal requests, such as asking to keep this or take that sentimental object. You may feel uncomfortable, but if the seller is determined to put you in this awkward spot, always say that the seller will have to have his or her attorney put that question in writing. Otherwise you could end up listening to a pleading seller who might distract you from your primary purpose, which is to inspect the house.

We're buying a brand-new house. Do we need a pre-closing inspection?

Yes. New doesn't always mean perfect. Have an inspector look for cracking in the staircases or window frames; such cracking can happen as a new foundation settles. Also, you and the developer should have come to an agreement on what will be included in your new home. Have the developer put everything in writing, and bring that list with you when you go to your preclosing inspection.

Our closing is a week away and the developer still hasn't treated the wood floors. I don't want to delay the closing, but I really need the developer to finish up this job. What should I do?

I'm sorry to say that this situation is fairly common with new houses. Developers often work right up until the last minute to complete a job, and certain tasks may actually be completed on the day of the closing. During your preclosing inspection make a list of all unfinished work, and give this list to your real estate agent or lawyer. He or she will present this list to the developer and ask that these tasks be completed before the closing. This way the onus falls on the developer to complete the job he agreed to under contract and, assuming that he needs more time, you are not the party asking for an extension on the closing date.

The seller had a brass mirror hanging on one of the walls. I didn't want it, but now that it has been taken down, there is a rectangular stain outlining where the mirror hung. Can I make the seller repaint the wall?

Making the seller pay for damages and/or missing items of this nature is tricky. The best way to deal with a situation like the one you've described is to present your real estate agent and your attorney with the problem. They will present the problem(s) to the seller's attorney and real estate agent and ask that the issue be resolved before the closing.

Just because you include a problem on your list doesn't mean the seller will pay for or remedy it, but your requests, if they are legitimate, may put some pressure on the seller. Remember, as eager as you may be to close on and own the house, a seller who has come this far with you (and who may be purchasing another home dependent upon the sale of this one) is just as anxious to close the deal.

CLOSING COSTS

What are closing costs?

Closing costs may include the following: loan application fees (if not already paid), lender's points, prepaid homeowner's insurance, an appraisal fee, escrow fees, lawyer's fees, recording fees, title search and insurance, tax adjustments, agent commissions, and PMI (if necessary). On average, these costs range from 2 to 4 percent of your total purchase cost, depending on where in the country you live.

How can I get an estimate of what my closing costs will be?

By law, your lender must give you a "good faith" estimate of your closing costs within three days of receiving your application for a loan.

These fees are a little confusing. Could you give me an approximate breakdown of what to expect for each of the major categories?

Yes. Here's a list of costs. Please note: They represent the high end of the spectrum, so your costs may be smaller.

- Credit Report: Most credit reports cost about $25, which includes the bank's markup. All lenders run credit checks on their applicants.
- Loan Application Fee: Unbelievable as it may seem, many lenders charge you to apply for a loan. The going rate is between a few dollars and a few hundred dollars—make sure you ask.
- Independent Appraisal Fee: The lender wants to make sure its loan is in keeping with the value of the purchase. Therefore, an independent appraiser must estimate the value of your home. The cost of an independent appraisal is approximately $343 on average.
- Lender's Points: This is the charge that the lender imposes in connection with the loan. A point is equal to 1 percent of the loan amount. On a mortgage of $200,000 with 1 point, the figure would be $2,000.
- Title Search and Insurance: You and the lender want to be sure the title to your future home is free of any liens and that the seller can give you a clear title. Title insurance costs from $500 to much more.
- Processing fee: This one is a little hard to swallow. The lender charges you to process the paperwork for your loan. This is different from the application fee, and will run about $380 on average.
- Preparation fee: Yes, the lender may charge you to prepare all the paperwork as well. This will cost another $200 to $300.

- Prepayment of Interest: Depending on the time of the month you buy the house, you will have to come up with an amount of money to prepay the interest on your mortgage until the loan closes. Assuming a $200,000 mortgage at 6.5 percent and 15 days of prepaid interest, that will come to about $534.

With those costs alone, you're nearing $4,000, and there will probably be others. Normally, there are transfer taxes, mortgage taxes, recording fees, real estate tax escrow, escrow fees, insurance escrow, inspection fees, attorney's fees, agent's fees, and others that are labeled junk fees. On average, the closing costs for a $200,000 mortgage are about $5,000.

My uncle told me to fold some of my closing costs into the mortgage itself. Is this financially wise?

No. I will give you one fundamental piece of advice that applies to most financial decisions such as this: Never pay tomorrow what you can afford to pay today. Why? In the case of a 30-year, $200,000 mortgage at a 6.5 percent interest rate, $5,000 in closing costs will end up costing more than $11,378 over the life of the mortgage. Every month, you'll be paying out about $32 extra to carry that $5,000 over 30 years. If you invested that $32 a month at 8 percent for 30 years, you would have $47,692. That's a lot of money. Think long and hard about giving it up.

That said, if you plan to live in your new home for five years or less, folding in the closing costs may make sense for you.

Renting to the Seller

We are buying a house, and the sellers need to stay a month after the closing. What should we do?

When sellers need to stay beyond the closing date, draw up a rental agreement that establishes the date the sellers will move out. Add a substantial financial penalty for every day they remain in your house beyond that date (say, $1,000 per day). During the period of overlap, you'll be forced to carry two separate mortgages and/or rents: one for the new house you've bought from the seller, and another for the house you're still living in while they stay the extra month. Therefore, the sellers must be responsible for their share.

Your lawyer or real estate agent should know how to handle this situation.

Refinancing

All my neighbors have been refinancing their mortgages. What exactly is refinancing, and why do people do it?

Refinancing just means that you are replacing the current mortgage on your house with another mortgage of a different rate and/or size and duration. People who originally mortgaged their houses when interest rates were high often refinance to take advantage of lower rates. Basically, people refinance in order to decrease their mortgage payments or to pay off other current debts with the proceeds of the new mortgage. People who have an adjustable rate, or variable mortgage (on which the mortgage payments change as interest rates change) that they want to convert to a fixed-rate mortgage (on which the payments are the same over the life of the loan) may also want to refinance when interest rates get low.

Is refinancing my mortgage to help me pay down my other debt a bad idea?

Needing to refinance to pay other debts isn't the ideal position to be in, but there are times when it may be appropriate. If, for example, you plan to keep your home for at least the next few years *and* new interest rates are lower than the current interest rate on your mortgage or the interest rate on the debt that you owe, *and* the closing costs are minimal, refinancing may make sense for you.

What may *not* make sense is refinancing only to lower the balance on your credit card debt or other debt when you are increasing the interest rate on your mortgage. Also, take into account any closing costs you may have to pay when you refinance—they can be several thousand dollars. If you are thinking about refinancing in order to lower the payments on your current debts other than your mortgage, you might consider an equity line of credit instead, because you could avoid the higher closing costs.

I'm about to refinance, and I'm thinking about taking equity out of my home to pay off my credit card debt. Is this a good thing to do?

It can be a smart move, but only if you are very careful and very responsible. On the surface this looks like a terrific move because you are getting rid of credit card debt, where the interest payments aren't tax-deductible, and trading it for home equity debt, in which the interest payments are tax-deductible. But here's where you need to be careful and responsible. If you were to mess up and not pay your credit card bills, the worst that could happen is that your credit score would become mud and you would probably find it very difficult to get a credit card or a loan. But if you roll the debt into a home equity line of credit or loan, you now have a much bigger problem: If you miss your payments, you could lose your house. That's because your house is your collateral for the loan. If you can't pay the loan, the lender is going to want the collateral. Another problem is that by getting rid of your old credit card debt, you could tempt yourself to run up a lot of new debt. If you lack the self-control to manage your spending, be very careful about making this move, or at least ask the credit card company to lower your credit limit so there won't be any new problems.

Over the past few years, interest rates have gone up, but seem to be holding steady now. How do I know when it makes sense to refinance?

First, you need to take the amount of your current monthly mortgage payment and subtract it from the amount of your new monthly mortgage payment if you refinance. (There are tons of free online calculators that can help you with this comparison. One of my favorites is in the calculator section of *www.lendingtree.com.*) This will give you your monthly savings if you refinance. The next step is to see how long it will take you to recoup the cost of the refinancing. To do this, simply divide your monthly savings into your closing costs; that will show you how many months it will take to break even. For example, let's say you currently have a $2,000 monthly mortgage that you can refinance to $1,900. So we're talking about a $100 monthly savings. Now let's say your closing costs on the refinance are $2,000. If we divide $100 into $2,000 we're looking at a 20-month period until you break even. If you expect to stay in the house at least that long, then it's smart to refinance. But if you think you might be moving, then I would recommend sticking with your existing mortgage.

I'm 50 years old, I just refinanced my house, and I'll be retiring in twelve years. Should I pay off my mortgage or contribute everything I can to my 401(k) plan? My 401(k) plan does not match.

Given the high price of real estate, it is most likely that your biggest monthly expense is your mortgage payment. And in today's market environment, I think it will be very difficult for you to achieve a spectacular rate of growth on your 401(k) plan, generating enough income to pay your mortgage payment in retirement. So I am leaning toward paying off the mortgage. Let me explain why. Let's say you have a $130,000 mortgage at 5 percent for 15 years and your mortgage payment is $1,000 a month. For your 401(k) to generate $1,000 a month after taxes, you will need to accumulate approximately $450,000 in your 401(k) by the time you retire. If you had that much, and we assumed a 3.5 percent to 4 percent return, your 401(k) would generate about $16,000 before taxes and $12,000 after taxes. If you ask me, it is a lot easier to pay off the $130,000 mortgage over the next 12 years than to require your 401(k) to generate $12,000 in after-tax income when you are retired. So please pay off your mortgage first.

Do you suggest everyone pay off their mortgage early and not contribute to their 401(k) plans?

No, but when you're approximately 45 to 50 years of age, you finally know you are in a home you are going to stay in. And at that point, why not eliminate what is probably your biggest monthly expense? Your retirement will be all the more secure, knowing you can stay in your house without any mortgage worries.

If I refinance, can I take any points I pay off my taxes?

Yes, but the tax situation is different with refinancing than with taking out an original mortgage because the points you pay when you refinance can't be deducted from your taxes immediately in a lump sum; you spread the deduction out over the whole length of the mortgage. Say you refinance your home with a 15-year mortgage and pay $3,600 in points. The deduction on these points must be spread out evenly over the life of the loan. That means you can deduct $240 each year for 15 years. There's one exception. Let's say that two years into your mortgage, interest rates drop further and you refinance again. Now the balance of the points that you paid on the last mortgage is completely deductible. If you paid $3,600 in points two years ago and have deducted $480 of that off your taxes so far ($240 a year), you can deduct $3,120 this year. And, of course, you can also deduct the appropriate portion of your new points.

Is there anything else to keep in mind when I am thinking about refinancing?

It's very important to understand that when you refinance you are not only changing the rate of your loan but also could be adding years to your loan. For example, say you originally borrowed $150,000 for 15 years at 8.85 percent with monthly payments of $1,508. You have been making those payments for six years, so your remaining principal balance is $110,000. If you refinance only that $110,000 by getting another 15-year loan at 7 percent, your monthly payments will drop to $989, but you will also be adding six years to the life of the loan. You can figure out the total cost of your new mortgage over the next 15 years by multiplying $989 by 180 (the number of months in 15 years): You will be paying $178,020. To figure out the total remaining cost of your old loan, multiply your current monthly payment of $1,508 by 108 (the number of months in nine years) and compare: If you don't refinance, you're going to pay $162,864. As you can see, even though your monthly payments will be lower with the new mortgage, over time it will cost you $15,156 more—not including closing costs on the new mortgage.

So if I can afford my monthly payments, I really shouldn't refinance, since I'll actually be losing money by doing so?

Not necessarily. You still might want to refinance in order to take advantage of a lower interest rate, but if you do, consider increasing your monthly payments to at least the amount that will enable you to pay off your mortgage in the period of time remaining on your *original* loan. Using the figures in the example above, you would have to pay $1,376 every month to pay the loan off in nine years. You would be paying $132 less each month than you would have with your original mortgage, which over the next nine years ($132 multiplied by 108 months), adds up to savings of $14,256. Even if your closing costs cost a few thousand dollars, in this case refinancing would be worth it.

I'm about to refinance a 30-year mortgage I've had for four years. I don't really want to shorten the length of my mortgage to 15 years, but I don't want to go backward either. How can I avoid starting over at a full 30 years?

Here's an easy way. To use your example, let's say that four years ago you took out a 30-year mortgage for $200,000. Now, four years later, your balance is probably roughly $192,000. When looking to refinance, using the technique above, you'd probably refinance your existing balance of $192,000 at the lower rate, and you'd then have 30 years remaining on your new loan. But here's a neat trick. Instead of refinancing $192,000, you could refinance the original principal balance of $200,000. Then, when you go to the closing table, you'd pay the old mortgage company the $192,000 you owe them, leaving you with $8,000. If you take that $8,000 and prepay principal on the *new* mortgage, interestingly, that puts you in precisely the same spot on the mortgage amortization schedule that you were in before you refinanced. You'd only have 26 years left to pay.

This strategy works with any loan amount and any payment period. One caveat: If your new mortgage has a prepayment penalty—which is rare, but they do exist—then it may not work for you.

What are the advantages and disadvantages of refinancing my 30-year mortgage as a 15-year mortgage?

The benefits are huge. The only real disadvantage is that your monthly payment will go up, relative to the payment on a 30-year loan—though probably not by as much as you think.

Here are a couple of things to keep in mind about a 15-year mortgage. First, just because you are paying off the loan in half the time of a 30-year mortgage doesn't mean that your payments will be twice as high. As a rule of thumb, payments on a 15-year mortgage are typically only about 25 percent higher than on a 30-year mortgage.

One reason for this "discount" is that the interest rate you pay with a 15-year loan is usually about .5 percent lower than with a 30-year loan. So if you take out a 30-year, $200,000 mortgage, for example, you might pay 6 percent, resulting in a monthly payment of $1,199; if you took out a 15-year, $200,000 mortgage, you'd probably get a rate closer to 5.5 percent, for a monthly payment of $1,634—only about 25 percent higher. And because you'll be paying off the 15-year loan faster, a greater portion of every payment you make will go toward your principal, so you'll be building equity more quickly. At the end of 15 years, you will own your home outright.

Yet you don't have to wait the full 15 years to see a big benefit. Five years down the road you will have built up a lot more equity in your home than you would with a 30-year option. In fact, the benefits of the shorter term start accruing instantly, though you may not realize this until you go to refinance again or decide to take some equity out of your home—either to buy a new home or for an important expense, like your child's college education.

If I can't afford a 15-year mortgage, is there another good option?

Yes. If the monthly payments on a 15-year loan are too high, look into a 20-year loan. Surprisingly, the payment differential between a 20-year and a 30-year loan is only about $100 a month for every $100,000 you borrow.

Here's where this tactic can come in handy. Oftentimes, when I arrange refinancing for a client, the amount the client is going to save because of a lower rate is just about the same amount as that monthly differential—say, $200 a month on a $200,000 mortgage. Now, the client can either take that extra money and, quite frankly, spend it on incidentals—which many people do—or consider refinancing at a 20-year term and keeping the monthly payment pretty much the same. You won't miss the extra monthly cash you never pocketed, and there's a tremendous benefit in terms of building equity and owning your home more quickly.

What are the other advantages of choosing a 15- or 20-year mortgage?

There are two big potential advantages that people may not know about.

One is that a shorter amortization term creates a potential savings on private mortgage insurance, or PMI—which you typically have to pay when you take out a loan with a down payment of less than 20 percent. If you choose a 15- or 20-year loan, the amount of PMI you have to pay is dramatically reduced, because the loan is considered less risky; plus, you reach your equity threshold more quickly, so you eliminate the PMI at an earlier stage.

The second benefit occurs if you take out a 15-year or 20-year adjustable-rate mortgage (ARM). Now, I know that people typically choose an adjustable-rate mortgage because they want a smaller initial monthly payment. But sometimes people truly have an option—they can afford a larger payment, but the ARM appeals to them because they're planning a move in, say, five to seven years and want to pay the smallest amount of interest possible in the meantime. If you go for a 15- or 20-year ARM, as opposed to a 30-year ARM, the chances are that your initial guaranteed interest rate will be lower—that's number one. Number two is that your equity buildup will accelerate. And here's where it gets interesting: Because you will have paid off more principal, when your ARM does come due for an adjustment, even if your rate rises, the difference in your monthly payments will be less because your loan balance will be lower.

I have a little vacation home that I am still financing. Do you recommend refinancing a second home?

Actually, I recommend refinancing your main home because the mortgage rates—including refinanced rates—on second homes or rental properties tend to be higher than on a primary home. If you have enough equity in your primary residence, investigate refinancing it for the purpose of paying off the other property. You may be able effectively to consolidate your debt at the lower interest rate.

Equity Lines of Credit

If I don't want to refinance because interest rates have risen, is there any other way to gain access to the equity I've built up in my home?
Yes. You can either take a home equity line of credit or a home equity loan. Because most people take such a loan or line of credit to pay back past debt or prevent future debt on such things as renovations, more information appears in *Ask Suze . . . About Debt*.

What is an equity line of credit, and who should consider using one?
An equity line of credit is a preset maximum amount of money that a lender is willing to allow you to borrow, based on the current available equity in your home. You may tap this line of credit any time and in any way you like, usually by simply writing a check. You do not pay interest until you use the money, and you will pay interest only on the amount that you actually use. Please note that you may choose *never* to use the line of credit. In many cases the interest rate fluctuates. Typically, it is not fixed, and neither is the payback period.

A home equity loan, on the other hand, is a lump-sum loan that comes with a fixed interest rate and, in most cases, a fixed payback period.

Before you apply for an equity line of credit against your home, you have to have an adequate amount of income and a certain level of equity already paid in to your house, as determined by your lender's standards. Assuming you meet the basic qualifications, a home equity loan *may* make sense for you if you need money for only a short period of time (a few years, maximum), if you are planning to sell your home within two years but you need some extra cash now, if interest rates are projected to fall, if you need to secure a source of funds in case of an emergency, or if you want to lower the interest rates on your other debts but not on your mortgage.

Do you recommend an equity line of credit or a refinancing strategy when interest rates are low?

As a general rule, you don't want to take out an equity line of credit if you need to use the money over a long period of time, because the interest rates on equity lines fluctuate. Therefore, if you are going to need the money for a long time, the bank is offering you low closing costs, and interest rates are low, refinancing at a fixed rate makes more sense, but be careful of prepayment penalties.

Refinancing is a good plan only if you are going to be staying in the house for at least as long as it takes to recoup the costs of refinancing. If you are planning to sell the house within two years, an equity line of credit is the better choice.

Is the reverse true in a high-interest-rate environment?

A home equity line of credit is the smarter move if interest rates are high and expected to fall. Since, again, the interest rates on most equity lines are variable, you will benefit when rates fall.

There is no way I'm going to qualify for another mortgage or an equity line of credit, because we ran into some bad times recently and our credit is terrible, not to mention the fact that our house is actually declining

in value. But we really can't make our payments. Is there anything we can do?

If you are at the end of your financial rope and there is no one in your life who could loan you the money to straighten things out, I would suggest calling your mortgage company and asking if it would consider offering you a hardship case reduction of interest. It is in the lender's interest to do this because the lender would find it as difficult as you would to sell a property that is decreasing in value. Of course, this will work only if the interest rate you are paying is higher than current interest rates.

PAYING OFF YOUR MORTGAGE

I'm planning to retire in five or six years and don't have much money. My sister says I should not pay off my mortgage early because it is a good tax deduction and because I could be making more by investing the extra money for growth in the stock market. Do you agree?

Your sister's points would be valid if you had plenty of money to meet your monthly expenses and invest. But if you are making up for lost time in your retirement planning, tax deductions may not save you over the long run. Also, don't forget that as time passes, the portion of your monthly mortgage payment that goes to pay off interest—the part that gives you the deduction—gets progressively smaller. Finally, if money is tight because you don't have much income, taxes are not your biggest problem.

About investing the money more productively somewhere else, it is true that you might make a better return in stocks, and if you can, you should. But you might also do worse. If you remember that your retirement income will largely be fixed and that you may have difficulty meeting high monthly expenses, paying off your mortgage could be a smart move to provide security.

If your current investments are not consistently earning as high a return as the interest rate you are paying on your mortgage, paying off the mortgage could be an excellent move.

Why is paying off the mortgage quickly a good move if I'm worried about my income when I retire?

Paying off your mortgage eliminates one of your biggest monthly expenses and allows you to make the most of the income you have. Imagine that you have just retired and are having a little trouble living on the fixed income available to you. For about ten years, you have been living comfortably in a house that you financed with a 30-year mortgage of $150,000 at a fixed rate of 7 percent. Your monthly payment is $998, and you have 20 years to go. What can you do to be more financially secure in this situation? You can go back to work, you can make sure that whatever money you have is earning the highest rate of return safely possible, you can reduce your expenses, or you can combine these strategies.

Returning to work could be highly impractical for you, even if you are still healthy and strong. Plus, there is a huge difference between wanting to work and having to work, and I'm sure you don't want to spend your retirement years forced to work. In terms of investing, if you are at or near retirement age, your best bet is going to be something that yields a nice safe dividend or interest income, which could give you a few hundred dollars each month but probably not enough to pay the mortgage, unless you have saved a hefty amount of money. Finally, trimming your expenses during your retirement years can be difficult—there are only so many things you can reduce or cut out.

If you are concerned about money after you retire, if you want to keep living in your home, and if you don't have current credit card debt, you might well want to pay off that mortgage as soon as possible, with the goal of having it paid by the time you retire. Ask your lender to estimate the additional amount of money necessary to pay off your mortgage in the number of years between now and your retirement.

I am getting ready to retire and have some savings— enough to pay off my mortgage in full. Should I do that, or just keep paying monthly?
Assuming that your savings are not entirely held in retirement accounts and that there will not be a substantial tax burden when you liquidate them, I think that if you have the money available to pay that mortgage off in full right now, and your income is not high enough to make the mortgage tax deduction worth it, you should consider doing this. You could substantially increase your cash flow. Here's why:

Let's say you have 20 years and $128,718 left to pay on a $150,000 fixed-rate mortgage that you borrowed at 7 percent (a $998 payment each month). We'll also assume that you will get Social Security but not a pension, you have $200,000 in a money-market fund earning 5 percent, and you have a modest retirement account, but not much else. Finally, we'll say that you are single and in the 15 percent tax bracket. We won't take the taxes owed on the money you earn in the money-market fund and the taxes saved on the interest for the mortgage into consideration, because they effectively cancel each other out. (Your tax savings on the mortgage would be $1,366 and the taxes owed on the money market interest would be $1,500, so we'll call that even.)

Now, I understand if your instinct is to hold on to that $200,000 in the money-market fund, because having a nice chunk of money in the bank makes everyone feel safe. But sometimes you can jeopardize your financial safety by letting money sit in the bank instead of using it wisely. If that money-market fund with the 5 percent interest rate is generating about $10,000 each year, or $833 each month, and you add to it $165 each month from your Social Security check, that's enough to make your mortgage payment each month.

But consider this: If you take $128,718 out of the money-market fund and pay your mortgage off completely, you will have $71,282 left in your money-market account, which should generate $297 each month at that 5 percent interest rate. And even though your interest income is reduced from $833 to $297 each month, you have no mortgage payment, so your monthly expenses have dropped by $998. If you think about it, there really is no comparison.

I think your goal should be to have paid off your home by the time you begin to receive Social Security. At that point, your expenses will be reduced by whatever the amount of your mortgage payment was, and your income will be increased by your Social Security benefit.

I don't know how secure I would feel not having more cash in the bank. What if something happens and I need the money?

Remember, your money has not disappeared into thin air. It is, effectively, in your home, which, in certain circumstances, may be a safer place for it than a stock mutual fund or other kinds of assets. Think about what kind of "somethings" are likely to happen to you. One possibility is that you might have to go into a nursing home. If you don't have long-term care insurance or other nursing home coverage, you would have to spend almost all your cash before you would qualify for Medicaid. But many states view your home as an exempt asset when you are qualifying for Medicaid, no matter how much equity you have in it. In other words, in many states, you can qualify for Medicaid and still own your house. Also, if you ever need extra income, you can get that through a reverse mortgage, which you do not have to qualify for.

My bank wants me to take out a biweekly mortgage, saying that it will reduce my current mortgage by eight years and it will not cost me one extra penny. Should I do this?

The bank is not being truthful. The biweekly mortgage will cost you more, because you are sending in one more payment a year on the biweekly than if you stuck with the monthly. That is why it reduces your mortgage. In addition, most banks will usually charge a $300 setup fee and $5 every time you make a payment. You can accomplish the exact same thing without any of those extra fees by simply sending in one extra payment yourself. If you do, it will reduce a 30-year mortgage to 22 years and a 15-year mortgage to 12 years. If you do want to send in an extra payment, check with your lender to see if your mortgage allows for this "prepayment." If it doesn't, you will be hit with an early prepayment fee. The only time it makes sense to pay the bank to do it for you is if you are not disciplined enough to do it on your own—then it is a wise investment to take out a biweekly mortgage.

REVERSE MORTGAGES

A reverse mortgage is a special kind of mortgage loan sometimes used by older Americans to convert the equity they hold in their homes into cash that they can use to live on. If you have equity in your home and if cash is tight and you need a source of income, this can be a useful tool to help provide financial security in your retirement years.

A reverse mortgage is aptly named. The payment stream is literally "reversed"—instead of you making monthly payments to a lender, as you do with a conventional mortgage or home equity loan, a lender makes payments to you, based on the amount of equity you hold.

How do I qualify for a reverse mortgage?

You must be at least 62 years old and own your home or condominium. You may be eligible even if you still owe money on a first or second mortgage. In fact, many older Americans get a reverse mortgage to help pay off their first mortgages. There are no income or medical requirements.

How much money can I get on a reverse mortgage?

The maximum size of your reverse mortgage will depend on your age at the time you apply, the kind of reverse mortgage you choose (more about this below), the value of your home, how much equity you have in it, current interest rates, and sometimes where you live. In general, the older you are, the more valuable your home, and the less you owe on it, the larger the potential income from the reverse mortgage will be.

Does the income from a reverse mortgage have to be paid back?

Yes, it does, but payments are not due while you are still living in your home. The loan, plus the interest you are paying on the loan, come due only when you no longer occupy your home as a principal residence. This typically occurs when you (or your spouse, in case you are married) pass away, sell your home, or permanently move out.

What if my family does not want to sell the home when I die, but wants to keep it?

They won't be forced to sell the home to pay off the loan. You or your family can pay off the reverse mortgage and keep the home.

What can the money from a reverse mortgage be used for?

It can be used for anything you like: daily living expenses, medical costs, home repairs or improvements, long-term health care, to pay off debts or prevent foreclosure on your home, or even travel.

Are there different ways to take the money from a reverse mortgage?

Yes. The options for taking your money are: all at once (lump sum); fixed monthly payments (for a period up to life); a line of credit; or a combination of a line of credit and monthly payments. The most popular option—chosen by more than 60 percent of borrowers—is the line of credit, which allows you to draw on the loan proceeds at any time.

Are there different kinds of reverse mortgages?

Yes. There are three basic kinds—FHA-insured, lender-insured, and uninsured. Although the FHA- and lender-insured plans appear similar, there are important differences.

What is an FHA-insured reverse mortgage?

FHA stands for Federal Housing Administration, a quasi-government agency that, as an insurer of reverse mortgages, guarantees that you will continue to receive your money even if a lender defaults. This kind of reverse mortgage offers a monthly payment amount plus a line of credit. As with other reverse mortgages, the mortgage amount is not due as long as you live in your home. Closing costs, a mortgage insurance premium, and sometimes a monthly servicing fee are required. Interest is charged at an adjustable rate on your loan balance; any changes in the interest rate charged affect how quickly your loan balance grows over time, not the amount of the monthly payments you receive.

FHA reverse mortgages may provide smaller loan advances than lender-insured plans.

What is a lender-insured reverse mortgage?

A lender-insured reverse mortgage is insured by the lender and typically offers a monthly payment amount or a monthly payment amount plus a line of credit. The interest you pay may be charged at a fixed rate or an adjustable rate, and additional loan costs can include a mortgage insurance premium (which may be fixed or variable) and other fees.

There are advantages to lender-insured plans. The amount you borrow may be larger than the amount you can borrow from an FHA-insured plan, and you may also be allowed to mortgage less than the full value of your home (thus preserving home equity for later use by you or your heirs). However, these loans may involve greater loan costs than FHA-insured or uninsured loans. Higher costs mean that your loan balance grows faster, leaving you with less equity over time.

Some lender-insured plans include an annuity that continues making monthly payments to you even if you sell your home and move. The security of these payments depends on the financial strength of the company providing them, so be sure to check the financial ratings of that company. Annuity payments may be taxable and affect your eligibility for Supplemental Security Income and Medicaid. These "reverse annuity mortgages" can also include additional charges based on any increases in the value of your home during the term of your loan, so check the provisions of such a loan carefully.

What is an uninsured reverse mortgage?

An uninsured reverse mortgage is dramatically different from an FHA- or a lender-insured reverse mortgage. An uninsured plan provides monthly payment amounts for a fixed term only—a definite number of years that you select when you first take out the loan. Your loan balance becomes due and payable when the payments stop. Interest is usually set at a fixed interest rate, and no mortgage insurance premium is required.

If you consider an uninsured reverse mortgage, think carefully about the amount of money you need monthly, how many years you may need the money, how you will repay the loan when it comes due, and how much remaining equity you will need after paying off the loan.

If you have short-term but substantial cash needs, the uninsured reverse mortgage can provide a greater monthly advance than the other plans. However, because you must pay back the loan by a specific date, it is important that you have a reliable source of repayment. If you are unable to repay the loan, you may have to sell your home and move. In most cases I do not like this kind of reverse mortgage.

What are the most popular kinds of reverse mortgages?

The most popular reverse mortgage is the FHA reverse mortgage called the Home Equity Conversion Mortgage Program (HECM). Other popular ones include the Home Keeper reverse mortgage, which was developed in the mid-1990s by Fannie Mae, a national mortgage company. A "jumbo" private reverse mortgage product offered by Financial Freedom Senior Funding Corp. of Irvine, California, is called the Cash Account Plan. The HECM and Home Keeper are available in every state, as is Financial Freedom's Cash Account Plan.

Does my home have to be in good condition to qualify for a reverse mortgage?

Yes. Your home must be structurally sound, meaning that there are no major defects, such as a bad foundation, a leaky roof, or termite damage. Once you have filled out a loan application, the lender will send an inspector to your home. If defects are found during the inspection, you will be responsible for finding a certified home improvement contractor who will make the necessary repairs.

If you don't have enough money to pay the contractor out of your own bank account, you can use a portion of the reverse mortgage money to pay for the home repairs.

After closing on your reverse mortgage, you have up to one year to complete the repairs. The lender who closed your loan will call you from time to time to check on the progress of the repair job.

Do I have to pay taxes on the money I get from a reverse mortgage?

No. Reverse mortgages are considered loan advances and are not taxable.

Does the money I get from a reverse mortgage affect my Social Security, Medicare, Medicaid, or SSI benefits?

No, the payments you receive from a reverse mortgage will not affect your Social Security or Medicare benefits. If you receive Supplemental Security Income, reverse mortgage advances will not affect your benefits as long as you spend them within the month you receive them. In most states, this is also true for Medicaid benefits. When in doubt, check with a benefits specialist at your local agency on aging.

How much will it cost to take out a reverse mortgage?

The costs of getting a reverse mortgage can include an origination fee (which can usually be financed as part of the mortgage), inspection and appraisal fees, and other charges similar to those for a regular mortgage.

What institutions offer reverse mortgages?

Reverse mortgages are offered by banks, savings and loans, and other financial institutions.

What can I do to protect myself against getting a bad reverse mortgage?

One of the best protections you have with reverse mortgages is the federal Truth in Lending Act, which requires lenders to inform you about the plan's terms and costs. Be sure you understand them before signing. Among other information, lenders must disclose the annual percentage rate (APR) and payment terms. On plans with adjustable rates, lenders must provide specific information about the variable-rate feature. On plans with credit lines, lenders also must inform you of any charges to open and use the account, such as charges for an appraisal, a credit report, or attorneys' fees.

You should know one more thing before applying for a reverse mortgage: You must first meet with a reverse mortgage counselor. A reverse mortgage lender can provide you with the names of approved counseling agencies in your area. A list of approved counseling agencies nationwide is posted on the Web by the U.S. Department of Housing and Urban Development (*www.hud.gov/offices/hsg/sfh/hecm/hecmlist.cfm*). The counselor's job is to educate you about reverse mortgages, to inform you about other options available to you given your situation, and to assist you in determining which reverse mortgage product would best fit your needs.

CAPITAL-GAINS TAX

The capital-gains tax rules on selling a home have improved dramatically in recent years. Here's what you need to know.

What is capital-gains tax and how does it affect the selling of my house?

Capital-gains tax is the tax payable on a gain resulting from the sale of a security or property that you have held longer than 12 months. Say you are a single person and bought your house 15 years ago for $100,000. Since then, you have put $20,000 worth of improvements into the house, and now you are about to sell it for $375,000, after fees and commissions. Your cost basis is the original price that you paid for the house plus the amount that you spent to improve it—in this case, $120,000 ($100,000 plus $20,000). You will owe capital-gains tax on the amount for which you sold the house minus all fees ($375,000), less your cost basis ($120,000), which is $255,000. However, every individual taxpayer is now entitled to a federal $250,000 exemption on a principal residence if they qualify, so you may be able to subtract $250,000 from $255,000. The result is that you may owe federal capital-gains tax on only $5,000 of your profit.

And now, with the passage of the Jobs and Growth Tax Relief Reconciliation Act of 2003, the capital-gains tax rate is

TAX RATES ON NET CAPITAL GAINS

ORDINARY TAX BRACKET	2003–2007	2008*
10% and 15%	5%	0%
All others	15%	15%

*After 2008, tax rates revert to pre-2003 act law.

only 15 percent (reduced from 20 percent in previous years) or 5 percent if you are in the 10 or 15 percent ordinary tax bracket. The 5 percent rate will be zero percent in 2008. For tax years after 2008, capital gains will be taxed as they were before the 2003 Act.

If I'm married, can my spouse and I each take a $250,000 exemption?
Yes, so if you're married and meet the tax requirements you have, in essence, a $500,000 exemption. In the above example, you would not owe any capital-gains tax if you were married.

How do I qualify for this exemption, and can I take it every time I sell a house?
You can take the exemption every two years, but keep in mind that it applies only if you are selling your primary residence. You need to have lived in a home as your primary residence for at least two of the last five years in order to qualify for this exemption.

If I buy a home, how much can I expect that home to increase in value every year?
That is a hard question to answer. The end of the 20th century brought double-digit annual returns to quite a few regions of

the country. Historically speaking, however, the nationwide average rate of growth in the value of a home is about 5 percent a year. Please note: Increased value will really depend on your location, as well as interest rates and economic conditions.

TRANSFERRING TITLE
TO THE CHILDREN

Now that I am getting older, would it be a good idea to transfer the title of my home to my daughter to avoid estate taxes as well as probate fees?

Depending on your financial goals and your estate-planning strategy, there are instances in which transferring the title of your house into your child's name may be a smart move, but it can also easily backfire.

First of all, if you give your house to your daughter, you will need to file a gift tax return to be used against your unified credit, or the amount of money or property you can leave to your beneficiaries without incurring gift or estate taxes. (For more on "gifting," please see *Ask Suze . . . About Wills and Trusts.*)

That said, with a gift, your daughter gets your cost basis on the home. With an inheritance, her tax basis is the fair market value at your death. So, making a gift could save considerable capital-gains taxes if your home has gone up in value. On the other hand, if your daughter were to get into any financial difficulty—if she were sued, for example, and someone won a judgment against her, or if she got involved in a nasty divorce—your house (which is now technically her house) would be vulnerable, which would threaten your own security. Also, if you ever needed the extra income you could get from a reverse mortgage, unless your daughter, who would hold title to the property, is older than 62, you would not be eligible to apply.

If my parents have put my name on their title and I want to take my name off it, how do we do that?

Very, very carefully—for you have to take into consideration the effect this will have on estate taxes. When your parents put your name on the title, they effectively gave you a gift of a portion of the house—let's say half. If the house at that time was valued at $800,000, they gave you $400,000 on paper and used up $376,000 ($400,000 less two $12,000 annual exclusions allowable under the gift tax law), or $188,000 each, of their respective $2 million in exemptions. (Exemptions rise to $3.5 million in 2009; there is no estate tax in 2010, but in 2011 the exemption goes back to $1 million unless Congress changes it.) If the house is worth $1 million when you give your half back to them, then *you* have used up $476,000 ($500,000 less two $12,000 annual exclusions) of your own estate tax exemption. If your parents were to die without having a death tax–saving trust (which would allow them to use both exemptions) and left you the entire house and all their assets—let's say the estate totals $2,600,000—you would owe estate taxes on $788,000, vs. $600,000 if they had not done this to begin with. Giving title back to them is going to cost you dearly in estate taxes, especially if the house continues to appreciate. Not to mention that you have now used up half of your own current estate tax exemption! If your parents' house is worth a lot of money, you should talk to an estate planner before removing your name from the title; this may help you to minimize the estate-tax consequences to you and your children.

REAL ESTATE AS AN INVESTMENT

Is real estate a wise investment?

If you are talking about simply buying a home to live in, then in my opinion it is probably one of the best investments you will ever make. Let me tell you why. Most home values appreciate 4 percent to 5 percent a year. Let's take a home that costs $100,000 (it does not matter how much homes are in your area—just increase or decrease the figure according to your area). With a typical 20 percent down payment, you will invest $20,000 in this house. Now let's assume that the house value appreciates 4 percent to 5 percent a year. That is a $4,000 to $5,000 increase on a $20,000 investment or a 20 percent return on your money. Where else are you going to get a 20 percent return on your investment today, have a home to live in, and get a tax write-off on the interest payments on your mortgage?

Friends of mine are encouraging me to invest in a real estate development, but I think the properties are overpriced. Any suggestions?

It was not a normal trend in 1999 when technology stocks and the overall stock market were going up by 25 to 80 percent a year. This kind of overvaluing has occurred in some areas of the country in real estate. This overvaluing of real estate is not normal either. Not many people wanted to admit that we had a real estate bubble forming. But whatever you call it, it's not normal when home prices rise that quickly. And when something is not normal, a correction almost always occurs to bring prices back in line with the normal rate of growth. By "correction," I mean that prices may go down for a while. This is what happened with the stock market after 1999, and this is what is likely to happen with overvalued real estate as well. So if you live in a part of the country where real estate is hyperinflated, I would advise you to be very careful about investing in real estate.

I'm not talking about buying a primary residence for you and your family to live in. That is one thing; there are advantages to this that may not be affected by a market bubble. But if you are thinking of buying investment real estate, that is another thing entirely. You must be very careful to know all that you need to known before you take the plunge.

ADDITIONAL RESOURCES

CREDIT REPORTS AND CREDIT SCORES

You can order a free annual credit report from each of the three nationwide credit reporting companies below by visiting their central website, *annualcreditreport.com*, or calling (877) 322-8228.

TransUnion
www.tuc.com

Experian
www.experian.com

Equifax
www.equifax.com

To find out your credit score, visit myFICO at *www.myfico.com*. The cost is $15.95.

MORTGAGES

For information from Fannie Mae about buying a home, call toll-free (800) 688-HOME or log on to *www.fanniemae.com/homebuyers*.

TITLE

American Land Title Association
1828 L Street, NW, Suite 705
Washington, DC 20036
(800) 787-ALTA
www.alta.org

This is the trade association for title companies. They can answer many questions about titling your property, and can give you the names of title companies in your area.

REVERSE MORTGAGES

The following information and publications may be obtained by mail, phone, or website.

Below are organizations and companies that provide general information about reverse mortgages or about reverse mortgage programs that they offer.

AARP Foundation
Washington, DC
(800) 209-8085 (AARP Reverse Mortgage Education Program)
www.aarp.org/rev/mort/list

This national nonprofit is an advocate for seniors and a source of consumer information on reverse mortgages.

Fannie Mae
3900 Wisconsin Avenue NW
Washington, DC 20016-2899
(800) 732-6643
www.fanniemae.com

This national secondary mortgage firm offers information on reverse mortgages, including HECMs and the mortgage products it offers. Consumers can call the toll-free number or contact their website to receive information, including lists of lenders.

Federal Trade Commission
Consumer Response Center
600 Pennsylvania Avenue NW, Room H-130
Washington, DC 20580-0001
(877) FTC-HELP (877-382-4357)
www.ftc.gov

The FTC has a publication titled "Facts for Consumers: Reverse Mortgages" that can be ordered over the phone or downloaded from their website.

Financial Freedom Senior Funding Corporation
19782 MacArthur Blvd., Suite 100
Irvine, CA 92612
(888) 738-3733
www.financialfreedom.com

This financial services firm has its own proprietary reverse mortgage products.

HUD (U.S. Dept. of Housing and Urban Development)
451 Seventh Street SW
Washington, DC 20410
(800) 225-5342 (for consumers)
(202) 708-2700 (Development Division, for lenders)
www.hud.gov

Operates the federal Home Equity Conversion Mortgage (HECM) reverse mortgage program. Their website has information about HECMs. The site also allows users to find out about approved FHA lenders that offer HECMs and the names of approved counseling agencies. Printed information can be obtained by calling the toll-free number above or visiting their website. In addition, the HUD Counseling Clearinghouse website offers information about HUD-approved housing counseling agencies and a list of agencies nationwide. The site also has the current FHA loan limits for the entire United States.

National Reverse Mortgage Lenders Association
1400 16th Street NW, Suite 420
Washington, DC 20036
(202) 939-1760
www.reversemortgage.org

This nonprofit organization is a source for consumer information on reverse mortgages.

FEDERAL HOUSING ADMINISTRATION

To find out the exact amount available for an FHA loan in your county, go to *www.hud.gov/fha/sfh/sfhhicos.html.*

To find your local FHA office, go to *www.hud.gov/local.html.*

HOME LOANS FOR VETERANS

Department of Veterans Affairs
(800) 827-1000
www.homeloans.va.gov

WEBSITES

FINDING A HOME ON THE INTERNET

www.realtor.com
www.buybankhomes.com

CORRECTING A CREDIT REPORT

www.tuc.com
www.experian.com
www.equifax.com
www.mycreditfile.com

MORTGAGE CALCULATORS

www.mtgprofessor.com
www.bankrate.com
www.interest.com/calculators

FINDING A BRAND-NEW HOME OR BUILDER

www.newhomenetwork.com
www.homebuilder.com

FINDING A REAL ESTATE AGENT

www.naeba.com
www.homegain.com
www.realtor.com

FINDING A MORTGAGE

www.lendingtree.com
www.eloan.com
www.realtytime.com
www.quickenloans.com
www.mortgageit.com
www.monstermoving.com

INDEX

INDEX

ABOUT SUZE ORMAN

SUZE ORMAN has been called "a force in the world of personal finance" and a "one-woman financial advice powerhouse" by *USA Today*. A two-time Emmy® Award–winning television show host, *New York Times* best-selling author, magazine and online columnist, writer-producer, and motivational speaker, Suze is undeniably America's most recognized personal finance expert.

Suze has written five consecutive *New York Times* best sellers— *The Money Book for the Young, Fabulous & Broke*; *The Laws of Money, The Lessons of Life*; *The Road to Wealth*; *The Courage to Be Rich*; and *The 9 Steps to Financial Freedom*—as well as the national best sellers *Suze Orman's Financial Guidebook* and *You've Earned It, Don't Lose It*. Her most recent book, *Women & Money*, was published by Spiegel & Grau in February 2007. A newspaper column, also called "Women & Money," syndicated by Universal Press Syndicate, began in January 2007. Additionally, she has created *Suze Orman's FICO Kit, Suze Orman's Will & Trust*

Kit, *Suze Orman's Insurance Kit*, *The Ask Suze Library System*, and *Suze Orman's Ultimate Protection Portfolio*.

Suze has written, coproduced, and hosted five PBS specials based on her *New York Times* best-selling books. She is the single most successful fund-raiser in the history of public television, and recently won her second Daytime Emmy® Award in the category of Outstanding Service Show Host. Suze won her first Emmy® in 2004, in the same category.

Suze is a contributing editor to *O, The Oprah Magazine* and *O at Home* and has a biweekly column, "Money Matters," on Yahoo! Finance. Suze hosts her own award-winning national CNBC-TV show, *The Suze Orman Show*, which airs every Saturday night, as well as *Financial Freedom Hour* on QVC television.

Suze has been honored with three American Women in Radio and Television (AWRT) Gracie Allen Awards. This award recognizes the nation's best radio, television, and cable programming for, by, and about women. In 2003, Suze garnered her first Gracie for *The Suze Orman Show* in the National/Network/Syndication Talk Show category. She won her second and third Gracies in the Individual Achievement: Program Host category in 2005 and 2006.

Profiled in *Worth* magazine's 100th issue as among those "who have revolutionized the way America thinks about money," Suze also was named one of *Smart Money* magazine's top thirty "Power Brokers," defined as those who have most influenced the mutual fund industry and affected our money, in 1999. A 2003 inductee into the Books for a Better Life (BBL) Award Hall of Fame in recognition of her ongoing contributions to self-improvement, Suze previously received the 1999 BBL Motivational Book Award for *The Courage to Be Rich*. As a tribute to her continuing involvement, in 2002 the organization established the

Suze Orman First Book Award to honor a first-time author of a self-improvement book in any category. She received a 2003 Crossing Borders Award from the Feminist Press. The award recognizes a distinguished group of women who not only have excelled in remarkable careers but also have shown great courage, vision, and conviction by forging new places for women in their respective fields. In 2002, Suze was selected as one of five distinguished recipients of the prestigious TJFR Group News Luminaries Award, which honors lifetime achievement in business journalism.

A sought-after motivational speaker, Suze has lectured widely throughout the United States, South Africa, and Asia to audiences of up to fifty thousand people, often appearing alongside individuals such as Colin Powell, Rudy Giuliani, Jerry Lewis, Steve Forbes, and Donald Trump. She has been featured in almost every major publication in the United States and has appeared numerous times on *The View*, *Larry King Live*, and *The Oprah Winfrey Show*.

A Certified Financial Planner®, Suze directed the Suze Orman Financial Group from 1987 to 1997, served as vice president of investments for Prudential Bache Securities from 1983 to 1987, and from 1980 to 1983 was an account executive at Merrill Lynch. Prior to that, she worked as a waitress at the Buttercup Bakery in Berkeley, California, from 1973 to 1980.